Rekindle Your Purpose

Revised Edition

**Break through
your disappointments,
discouragements, and detours to
resurrect your purpose**

AND LIVE IT!

Written by Diane Y. Chapman with Beth Sanden

*Cover Photo:
Beth Sanden is awarded first place
in the Rome Marathon 2014.*

Copyright © 2017

with 2018 Updates

Diane Y. Chapman and Beth Sanden

All rights reserved.

Published by Diane Y. Chapman

Book and Cover Design

by Diane Y. Chapman and Tiffany J. Adair

Beth is now listed in the

Guinness World Records

"The fastest aggregate time to complete a handcycle marathon on each continent (female) is 30 hr 12 min 31 sec, and was achieved by Elizabeth Sanden (USA) from 26 February 2012 to 11 June 2016."

and the
Official World Records

"First Handcycle Marathons on 7 Continents and the North Pole (Female)."

At 64 years old, paraplegic Beth Sanden breaks the barriers for all of us who have abandoned our dreams.

One race at a time, she is changing the world for us; the able-bodied, the disabled, the warriors who are wounded, the downtrodden, the frustrated, the "detoured," and those of us who feel our dreams have passed us by because of age or circumstance. And she's not finished.

Come along for a magnificent ride and learn how to set afire to who you are, ignite your sense of purpose, and break through to achieve what you are truly meant to do.

ENDORSEMENTS

"This book takes you inside the heart and soul of the amazing Beth Sanden. It's a journey you'll never forget. She was special before she was paralyzed in 2002. As a top age group triathlete and runner, she was training for an Ironman Triathlon when she was injured severely in a bike accident. The crash happened one week before she was to race in the legendary Boston Marathon. When life changes so abruptly and becomes the ultimate challenge, many people crumble. Not Beth. She realized her life would be different, but she had been given an opportunity to prove people wrong about the capabilities of disabled individuals. Her question was 'Why can't I still be an athlete?'

Not surprisingly she has done both. Beth has competed in countless triathlons and running events using her handcycle, and in 2010 went back to take care of unfinished business. She competed in the Boston Marathon. In between training and races, she visits local rehabilitation centers, giving hope and inspiration to other challenged athletes. After completing the 7 Continents Marathons, she went to compete in, and finish, the North Pole Marathon, and has yet more to come. In this book you'll look inside the amazing Beth Sanden."

-Bob Babbitt, Co-Founder, Challenged Athletes Foundation; USA Triathlon Hall of Fame Inductee; Ironman Triathlon Hall of Fame Inductee

"The more Beth accomplishes, the more she helps others. She is truly a guardian angel for challenged athletes. You'll see why."

- Bryon Solberg, MD

"This book about the inspirational life of Beth Sanden is a must-read. I guarantee it will give you the tools to live with confidence as you nurture your own dreams and purpose. You will be moved and motivated by her story."

- Judy Lang, Script Supervisor

"In this book, you will see how Beth is truly an inspiration. I met Beth when she raced her first Triathlon in Huntington beach. She wanted to know what exercises I did to get my calves looking so great!! We became close friends, and I remember the day she fell in the Guacamole Grande bike ride, and her immediate eight-hour surgery. In her rehabilitation, there were so many ups and downs, especially because of her terrible chronic pain. But she never let it stop her from getting back into life.

She has always been motivating others to do their best. Since the accident, she has been showing challenged and able-bodied people that no matter where you are and what challenges you have, you can always keep moving, keep improving, and do better. I absolutely love this lady."

- Kim White, Certified Life Coach, USA Triathlon Coach & Race Director, author of *365 Days to Abundant Health: The Little Steps to Help You Thrive*

"I have known Beth for 27 years. She turned an unhealthy fat 37 year-old lady (me) into a more fit and healthy 64 year-old who never thought she could do things she ended up doing. I competed in numerous run/walks from 5K to full marathons. I began ocean swims, and bicycle rides, and competing in triathlons. I feel younger now than I did at age 37 thanks to Beth! Read her story and you'll understand how she changed my life."

- Sachiko V. Fukumon, DDS

"Beth is a very special person, and this book is a wonderful read about her."

- Tom Hampton

> "Strength does not come from physical capacity. It comes from indomitable will." -
> Mahatma Gandhi

"Surviving is important. Thriving is elegant.
- Maya Angelou

DEDICATIONS

Diane:

My sister Susan Howington, who has always believed in my writing about people, and my ability to understand who they are, their hopes and dreams, and what they've overcome and achieved. She believes in the inspiration I strive to infuse into my writing and amongst all of my family, friends and clients. She and I are also very close, dear friends. She's such a blessing to me.

My brother Jim Chapman who has given me unconditional love all of my life. We have been through so much together, "partners in crime" during many explorations, and very close during life's experiences. He has always been there for me, and believes in me no matter what, and encourages my hopes and dreams.

My parents, Blair and Donna Skjerven Chapman, both deceased, but thought of every day of my life. They taught us to meet others with ease and enthusiasm, and indeed my father "never met a stranger." He found everyone he met to be interesting and worth a chat over coffee. They both encouraged me and my siblings to be receptive to new acquaintances of all backgrounds. Mom was very much a lady, and an amazing role model as a professional woman and a high school English teacher. She taught my sister and me to present ourselves as beautifully as possible every day. I've tried to live up to her example!

My two wonderful brothers who left this earth way too young. My brother Bill, who passed away at 23, and my brother Bob, who passed away at 47. There are no words to describe the void my two siblings and I feel day in and day out with our loss. We love them dearly and enjoyed them so much when they were with us.

Beth:

The Challenged Athletes Foundation (CAF) for granting my wish for a handcycle to go for some "unfinished business" at Boston Marathon 2010. Also for helping to get me to the start line in triathlons and marathons again.

The many friends I have made since becoming a part of the CAF family!

Achilles International for helping me to get into places I never thought I would be able to go.

For the many contacts I've been able to make around the world for marathons and for delivering excellent used equipment, with the help of CAF, to Achilles para-athletes in Italy, Africa and South America.

PossAbilities out of Loma Linda for helping me with a grant for the Antarctic Marathon.

Thank you to The City of San Clemente, and valuable friends too innumerable to name!

ACKNOWLEDGEMENTS

Our sincere thanks and appreciation to Tiffany J. Adair, without whom we would have been totally stumped about how to bring this book physically and electronically together.

Diane's acknowledgements:

My husband Mark Derengowski, who has watched me at my computer day after day, night after night, and often during times that we could be spending together. Throughout all of it he was understanding, even when my office was stacked high with notes and written pages scattered everywhere across the floor, like a bomb blast. I feel very blessed that we are celebrating our 20th year of marriage. Thank you so much for your love and patience, Mark.

My mother-in-law Fran Derengowski, 102 years old, who has been a wonderful mother to me; and my sister-in-law Eileen Disken, who easily became a great friend, along with being a great sister. Fran has eagerly awaited this book to be published. Both have been cheerleaders for me, and believers in my talents and abilities. It's wonderful to have them in my life.

All of my friends who have cheered me on to write and finish this story, expressing optimism about its future and the impact it will have on everyone who reads it. My thanks to Judy Lang, Missy McKinney, Nicki Herman, Karen Schaefer, Frank Mack, Diane McCraw, Nancy Santarelli- Gennaro, and Linda McIver, for being especially encouraging.

Beth's Acknowledgements:

I thank Christ for getting me through the seasons He's brought me through, and my loving husband, Burt, who stayed with me through the thick and thin of raising kids through a tumultuous spinal cord Injury and into a "new normal." Hope we didn't drown you in estrogen, Burt!

My two beautiful daughters, Brianna and Brooke, forgiving me the season of fallout. Thank you for choosing to stay in my life! My Mom, Rosalie, who visited day and night, lending a hand at "Camp Sanden," while helping to build the "new normal" with words of wisdom and loving touches, with an unwavering hand. She has been a bulwark in my life.

My numerous friends Elaine, Carol, Sachi, Ken, Kim, Gabrina, Evey, Katherine, Cheryl, Paul, Denise, Lissa, CAF, Fred, David, Sally, Lindi, Mel, Michelle, Hank, John, and Tom, who have supported me in many endeavors from rehab to the 7 Continents and North Pole Marathons.

FOREWORD

What could possibly be better than traveling the globe pursuing an ambitious multi-year goal to race the 7 Marathons on 7 Continents and the North Pole Marathon that ignites your innermost passions in life? How about doing all of that for a meaningful purpose and to benefit a cause far greater than yourself? This is exactly what Beth Sanden has done and has now chronicled in "Rekindle Your Purpose."

Anyone who has spent time with Beth is undoubtedly captivated by her infectious enthusiasm, contagious positive energy, strong drive and incredible spirit. My wife Denise and I have been fortunate to know Beth for nearly a decade and have collaborated with her on several endeavors to support and provide sports equipment to physically challenged athletes around the world.

Thanks to Beth our ability to personally deliver and present racing wheelchairs to some very special individuals in Africa and South America has added an unforgettable element to our mountaineering adventures on the seven continents. Beth says that our ascents of the Seven Summits (the highest mountains on every continent including Mt. Everest) are what inspired her to complete her remarkable record-setting quest.

To that I reply, Beth, the pursuit of your mission, your *rekindled purpose,* was growing inside of you for many years. Your story and example simply shed some sunlight at an appropriate time. It allowed your dream to grow and flourish into the wonderful reality that was destined to be realized no matter what, thanks to your unbounded faith, determination and true compassion for others.

Congratulations once again, Beth, on your amazing accomplishments. And for those who read these inspirational pages and aspire to do more, I wish you all the best on your journey, your own purposeful climb to live life to the fullest! Enjoy.

- Paul Fejtek, author of *Steps to the Summit, Reaching the Top in Business and Life*

PROLOGUE

Forget the notion that this is a book about a challenged athlete overcoming what some would call a disability. Beth Sanden's story is far more than that. It is food for the soul. It is inspiration. It is about how far the human spirit can carry us when we just apply courage, perseverance, hope and have faith in ourselves. You see, Beth Sanden isn't just an amazing person who triumphs over adversity. She is a life coach.

I have known Beth for more than a decade, and swam in her wake, cycled with her, and have run with her while she cranked her handcycle. I have witnessed Beth successfully and gently prove to a man in his seventies who had lost a foot that he could compete in half-Ironman events. I have seen her take a boy who could no longer walk and coach him into becoming a muscular and happy wheelchair athlete. But more than anything, I have seen Beth reignite the fire within both of these people.

As I write this, I am in sub-Saharan Africa and Beth Sanden is relatively close by pushing her way through a series of marathons -- day after day after day. Completing marathons in Africa may seem like no big deal, just as Beth taking on the Great Wall of China may seem like no big deal. But I am mountain biking. When debris on the Kalahari Desert gets in my way, I merely hop off my bicycle and walk. But Beth has no such luxury. On her heavy handcycle, she must figure out a way to get over, under, around or through every obstacle regardless of terrain, regardless of weather.

Yes, there are many things I have seen Beth do, that after this Ironman champion was paralyzed during a training bike ride more than a decade ago, doctors said she would never do. Heck, she even mastered marathons in the Antarctic, as well as at the North Pole. Yes, the North Pole.

As you read this book, you will learn how Beth never gives up on herself. You will find out why she doesn't give up on anyone. And best of all, you will find out how she coaches all of us to live our lives in full.

David Whiting

Metro Columnist, Orange County Register

Orange County, California

"Your future depends on many things, but mostly on you." - Frank Tyger

TABLE OF CONTENTS

Dear Reader 20
Introduction 26

Section One: Beth's Able Bodied Championship Racing

Chapter One: The Dream and the Journey 35
Chapter Two: Race Days in California and Kona!
Beth's Ironman Events 50

Section Two: After the Accident

Chapter Three: The Accident That Shattered
Her Spine and Her World 61
Chapter Four: Bouncing Back
and Resurrecting Her Dream..66
Chapter Five: Do You Long To Resurrect a Dream?
Or Start Over Again and Create Another?...............................75
Chapter Six: Triumphant on the Great Wall of China 93
Chapter Seven: Conquering 7 Marathons on 7 Continents ... 96
Chapter Eight: The North Pole Marathon 119
Chapter Nine: Beth's Commitment to Giving
Back To The World 132
Chapter Ten: How Can You Give Back in Your Own Life? 158
Epilogue: Joy and Purpose 164

DEAR READER,

This book has been a long time in the making. In fact, in a way, it's a book I wanted to start writing nearly 20 years ago, when Beth was able-bodied and had become a force to be reckoned with in the world of triathlon, marathon, and Ironman racing, after the age of 40. For those of you who are not familiar with racing, triathlons are broken into four categories:

- **A "Sprint" distance** includes a 500 to 800 yard swim; a 12 mile bike ride; and a 3.1 mile run.
- **An "Olympic" distance** is a 1500 yard swim; a 26 mile bike ride; and a 6.2 mile run.
- **A "Half-Ironman"** is a 1.2 mile swim; a 56 mile bike ride; and a 13.2 mile run.
- **A "Full-Ironman"** is a 2.4 mile swim; a 112 mile bike ride; and in case that's not enough for you, a full 26.2 mile marathon to top it off.

I don't know about you, but cheering from the sidelines would be good enough for me.

I have known Beth for more than 20 years, when we met as fitness professionals and enthusiasts. She was one of my favorite class instructors, and a personal trainer. I was a fellow credentialed fitness industry continuing education provider. I taught instructors and personal trainers the "promotional skills" part of the business; and Beth the exercise science and teaching skills. She invited me to participate in two of her exercise videos, and we team-taught fitness professionals throughout Southern California. We routinely carted around Beth's two young girls in the back seat, which usually amused me greatly, even though it led to their mother's frequent admonishments, much like the typical "If you two don't settle down, I'm going to pull over!"

No matter what happens in her life, Beth has always been a natural relationship builder. Her smile always lights up the room. I call it her "trademark." Always energetic, enthusiastic, always interested in those around her, always stopping for conversation, always connecting authentically with clients, neighbors, fellow race competitors, and friends.

We sat down one day and began what I thought would be a series of interviews with her to perhaps start a book. Beth wrote out for me a stream of consciousness about her initial foray into triathlon and marathon racing. She had begun a running club for some of her personal training clients, and wondered if racing would be something she'd be good at doing. She honestly didn't even know if she could. I find this humorous looking back.

As she "put her toe in the water" by training for running, biking, and swimming races, she realized that she loved it. It's a love affair that has not ended, as this book describes. As she progressed in her capabilities and started to win her races, she was encouraged by her racing comrades to try an Ironman competition. She did.

She was thrilled by the experience, and thrilled as well for her two daughters, for whom she believed her demonstrated willingness to put herself out there was incredibly important for them to see. She knew her actions spoke louder than words. Yes, it's trite, but, oh-so true. Her husband and girls were there, following her progress as she went the distance. After she crossed the finish line, she got the news that she had placed third in her age category. The next morning, she was awarded her trophy, and found out that she had earned an entrance into the holy grail of Ironman competitions: the Kona, Hawaii race.

As I mentioned above, I thought at that time there needed to be a book written about this amazing friend, who in her 40s became a racer known to everyone in the world of triathlon, marathon and Ironman racing. One day she realized, though, that her rigorous training and regular racing competitions had become more and more integrated into her life, fervently spilling into every "unused" minute outside of her full-time fitness career, motherhood, and wifehood, until she found herself arising every day by 4:30 AM to start 5:00 AM training. She loved it and pushed herself harder and harder and harder.

Finally, Beth called me one day and said, "Diane, it's not time for this book yet. It will be sometime, but it's not time yet." I understood. I knew her schedule, and how full her time had become. When I think back now, though, I wonder if something deep inside of her knew that another chapter in her life was coming, one that would touch the whole world with inspiration and hope for better lives. Perhaps a voice inside of her said, "Your life holds so much more to come."

I have had much joy writing this book, and hope you'll find limitless inspiration and motivation in it. It's been a labor of love. I find that in my own life there are more than a few moments when I need to be inspired, and to be reminded that I have a purpose to fulfill.

Whether it's in loving and accepting my family, nurturing my friendships, setting an example with my mostly healthy lifestyle, (Dang that midnight chocolate!) or using my talent of putting words together, I have a purpose. So do you, and this book is to help you find it, or resurrect it, and nurture it.

Sometimes we find that our purpose changes as we come to a crossroads in life, whether expected, or in Beth's case, completely unexpected. It's at these times, we must have faith that as one door closes, another opens, and our challenge is to refresh and "recalibrate." As Beth shows us over and over, we can still experience joy. It might take some time to find where it lies, but there is a kernel to cultivate somewhere. That kernel could be inside you. Let me point out, too, that when you do find it, perhaps your growth of purpose lies in helping someone else to get through a perfectly awful and overwhelmingly tough situation.

This book about my friend Beth was destined to be written, and I am honored to be the story teller. She is ready for the world to hear it. She overcame a horrific accident, hospitalization, paralysis, a dire prognosis, and relentless pain to walk again and to race.

Although a traumatic experience may seem like a lump of coal to you, to others who find themselves in the same or similar situation, your experience might be seen as gold. Your life could be the bridge from disappointment, discouragement and even despair to feeling inspiration once again.

It's in this spirit that I have added a few small chapters on finding inspiration and motivation from within yourself. I hope it will encourage you to take action in your own life to see the possibilities in your purpose, and perhaps act on them.

I have always found that taking action, whether in a big way or small, particularly to reach out to others in kindness, or even to *yourself* in kindness, reaps incalculable rewards. Taking a leap of faith to connect with others is life-changing to you and them.

And now, dear reader, I give you Beth Sanden, a one-of-a-kind human being, who shows us how to "rekindle our purpose" to break through our disappointments, discouragements, and detours to resurrect our purpose and live it. If she resurrected hers, under such horrendous circumstances, we can, too. Let's do it together. With heartfelt thanks for your readership,

Di Chapman

"You're not ever too old to set goals and reach them, able-bodied or disabled." - Beth Sanden

INTRODUCTION

If you are lucky in your lifetime, you will meet someone like Beth.

I'm talking about Beth Sanden, a 64-year-old paraplegic who is a global champion marathoner and triathlete contender, who has made a dramatic and inspirational impact worldwide.

And if you're truly blessed, you'll have the opportunity to know her for more than a few fleeting moments or chance encounters. I've had the privilege of knowing Beth for more than two decades. And God willing, I'll know her for many decades to come. With Beth in my life there are always lessons and blessings, there are always insights, and wisdom for troubling times that make me a better person from our time together. It always motivates me to be *more* of who I need to be to live vibrantly and fulfilled. Time with Beth gives me credits on the balance sheet of my personal P&L. It strengthens the compass I seek to calibrate one day at a time.

Beth is the real deal: genuine, quick to laugh, observant, and attentive. At the same time, she is contemplative, grounding, and careful with conclusions. A Registered Nurse by education, a fitness expert, Certified Personal Trainer, and Certified USA Triathlon Coach by vocation, she is well-versed in the "science" of life, skilled in the mechanics of our bodies, and faithful to research and evidence that guides her decisions.

Truth be told, she's very different than I, a creative soul who is quick to adopt superlatives, eager to "jump in with both feet," and constantly reaching for chocolate. I would have fit in perfectly with young Judy Garland and Mickey Rooney as they exclaimed in movie after movie, "Let's do a show! Let's do a BIG show!" Beth has always taken a more logical approach to life. But, nobody's perfect!

The fact is, Beth is all about "Go, go, go!" as well, but as a champion athlete, and not just any champion athlete, but as an athlete whose "calling" as a racer came not as a girl, but after her 40th birthday. She began her triathlon and marathon racing at 44 when she was able-bodied, and became a world-class competitor by 2001. She raced in the Ironman California, and the Kona Hawaii Ironman World Championship. She raced in the San Diego Rock and Roll Marathon, and qualified for the 2002 Boston Marathon.

But a tragic bicycle accident in April of 2002 interrupted Beth's plans to run in Boston. As she trained for another Ironman, participating in the Guacamole Grande bike race, a 50-mile race in Temecula, California, she suffered a terrible accident, and shattered the T6-7 vertebrae in her back like glass. It stabbed her spinal cord, which then leaked spinal fluid.

She underwent an eight-hour surgery. She was told she would never walk again.

Then, three days later, the pain started. Intense, stabbing, bright white hot central nervous system pain. "It was 50 times that of childbirth," she told me.

The pain continues to this day, and will be with her for the rest of her life.

Beth's story is of hope turned into grit, commitment, perseverance, faith, willpower, courage, and ultimately, joy. It will move you forward to achieve your own goals and dreams, and to overcome the obstacles that are sure to meet you on your journey.

The Beth I know turned this accident and pain, which was supposed to cripple her for the rest of her life, into a *"detour,"* not a nemesis.

It *changed* the champion in Beth to a purpose-driven competitor whose goal is to improve the world for all of us. The champion in her, who had to heal, and had to learn to live in a new body with constant pain, roared up to the challenge.

But wait. This is where it gets good. There is a magnificent twist to the story that overcomes the odds.

After months of hospitals, a body cast, going home to her children in a wheelchair, a second surgery 14 months after the first by a specialist in Colorado, and months more of limited movement, her husband and Ironman racing friends threw her into a swimming pool.

"You don't have legs, but you have arms," he said, knowing the competitor was still inside her. She swam every day. Her physical therapists used electrical stimulation on her legs to move over a treadmill. With determined willpower, within 18 months, she freed one leg from total to partial paralysis.

Now, using her arm strength, a cane, a walker, and a handcycle, Beth has been back in the race, back in the winner's circle, since 2004. She goes beyond the ability of many able-bodied triathlon and marathon contenders. Since the accident in 2002, and her painful recovery from a complete paraplegic to a *partial* one, as of this writing, Beth has competed globally in:

- **82 Marathons including**:

The North Pole Marathon
4 Boston Marathons
The "Seven Continents" Marathons (Yes, marathons on each of the seven continents!)

A "Triple 7" in Africa (As this book is published, Beth completed her "Triple Seven" in Africa: 7 marathons in 7 days in 7 different countries.)

- **78 Triathlons, Sprint, and Olympic distance**

She completed the Seven Continents series by racing in Vietnam in 2016. This year, she competed in and finished the ultimate marathon, the challenging, life-changing North Pole Marathon with 49 other competitors.

She races to win on behalf of the worldwide physically, emotionally, and mentally challenged population, including our warriors who are wounded who come home with PTSD, traumatic brain injuries, and loss of limbs; and the disabled who are ready to win their own literal and metaphorical "races" to integrate themselves back into life.

She is determined to show them to the world and help them choose to participate in life fully, and resurrect their dreams.

She also races on behalf of all of us who have been disappointed, discouraged and detoured from the path of our dreams and purpose because of age or circumstances. She is the perfect person to take on this role, after being brutally and abruptly injured, and distraught that she might never achieve the dreams she had as a racer.

Through her racing, she has raised funds to provide the disabled worldwide with handcycles and race wheelchairs, and has written letters for grantees for prosthetic limbs. Most of her races raise funds on behalf of the Challenged Athletes Foundation (CAF), who insures the delivery of equipment in the US and throughout the globe.

You will be astounded at the stuff she's made of - the stuff she's always been made of. It will become very clear to you why the path of her destiny unfolds. Her life has always had a calling. I've seen it spark, flicker, and ignite for over 20 years. I've seen her set the globe on fire. She is an inspirational role model for everyone. She has asked me to write this now because she is ready to spread the message:

"It is never too late to be what you might have been." - George Eliot

It's time for all of us to ignite our own sparks with a message about keeping the faith, overcoming adversity with strength of will, breaking through pain, and encouraging ourselves to persevere to win what we dream of in our lives. Words of encouragement, steps to fulfillment, the challenges of others, and timeless wisdom flow throughout the story.

This is about a champion, a tragedy, hopes crushed along with vertebrae, and the enormous willpower to rekindle her purpose - a story meant for us all.

Racing has become Beth's calling, her venue for her outreach to us to motivate us to stay on our quests, even as our challenges and traumas steer us off-course. Once you get to know her, you will understand why she is the perfect person to take on this role.

No matter who you are, no matter where you are, and no matter what you do in this world, you will learn lessons to share from the life of this unforgettable woman, for reasons that will move you, inspire you, and possibly even take your breath away.

She knows YOU can get back in your own race, too, breaking through your own challenges to rekindle your purpose. Be prepared to start the journey of becoming a "champion" in your life; better, stronger, and on the path to the person you truly dream to be.

> *"The best way to predict your future is to create it."*
>
> -Abraham Lincoln

BETH'S ABLE BODIED CHAMPIONSHIP RACING

"Excellence is not an act, but a habit."
- Aristotle

Chapter One:
The Dream and the Journey

A Busy Mom, Wife, and Fitness Professional Soon to be a champion racer.

"Nothing happens unless first a dream." - Carl Sandberg

"Where do you begin with a dream you've had for years and thought maybe it's impossible?" Beth asked me. "The sheer magnitude of the physical endurance required to compete in triathlons, and ultimately the Ironman competitions, overwhelmed me just considering them."

But she kept her wish to do both. She found the determination to commit to her dream. She knew the training would necessitate long hours away from home, riding a bicycle through hills, rock, and on sand at the beach, plus running and swimming daily. "I hadn't changed a flat or dealt with a slipped gear on a bike in years. The last time I rode was on one gear down to the beach and back!"

"I felt fortunate because I had support among family, my husband, my friends, and my work, a personal training and fitness studio. I was absolutely honored that the owners believed in me and offered to help me with entrance fees as well."

"The journey of a thousand miles begins with a single step. - Lau Tsu

Yes, I know you've seen this quote before, maybe dozens of times. But Beth discovered its truth. Her dream would come alive by starting with small steps. "I had to go from jogging to running. I hadn't had to go as fast as possible on a bike, with all gears engaged and ready to win. I really was no swimmer, but I could backstroke. Could I really pull this off?"

Beth was then averaging 30 hours a week as a fitness instructor and personal trainer for seven years. She was living her dream of helping others from all walks of life to adopt the healthy habit of exercise. She had formed a running club with clients, and among them she had Ironman competitors. One particular Ironman competitor, who was rehabilitating an injury with her, dared her to start doing triathlons. He had started in his 40s, and at the time she was 44 as well. She took the dare and never looked back. This was a woman who chased her dream, no matter what it took, but also did her best to be an attentive mother and wife. Could it be done?

As a working mother of two daughters, Beth's life was busy, full, and all-consuming, and as she says, "Any mother is busy, whether she has one child or ten."

She became a mom at 34, giving birth to daughter Brianna, and again at 36 when she and her husband adopted daughter Brooke as a newborn. Beth started working when Brianna was 18 months, building her fitness business. Brooke came shortly after, and fortunately, childcare was available at the gym, a common service started by the fitness industry because of a definite need by mothers who want to exercise. When she would travel to private homes to give personal training services, Beth used the classic age-old babysitting network of friends, sitters, and neighbors.

"I was and still am a working mom," says Beth, "and I have always wanted to influence my daughters by showing them what a woman can do to achieve her dreams."

She felt fortunate that her husband Burt was doing well in his business, and she could work part time and home school her children, at ages four and six. The girls then attended school at five and seven, in kindergarten and 2nd grade.

As she dedicated herself more and more to her dream, she talks of her husband as understanding, helpful at home with daily chores and the girls. "He's a great husband. He took over the bills, the kids, and some laundry along the way. He's a saint!" So, there's your answer. It can be done. It's a full family project of understanding and pitching in.

The Commitment

"Real courage is when you know you're licked before you begin - but you begin anyway and see it through no matter what." - Harper Lee

Yes, at 44, she started training for triathlons. She signed up for the Huntington Beach triathlon race. Hysterically, Beth was using an old bicycle to practice for races, laughing off any teasing it may have provoked. Unbelievably, when she began her search for a new one, she was told by a young salesman, "You're too old to do triathlons!" "He was serious!!" she says. So, she was off to another bike shop where the owner was so enthusiastic and helpful. She needed something affordable, and he had the perfect formerly-used, reconditioned bike for $200.

There is an enormous challenge in preparing for racing triathlons, marathons, and Ironman competitions. Triathlons include Ironman competitions, as they have the same format: swim, bike, run. In fact, once again, here are how triathlons are categorized:

- A "Sprint" includes a 500 to 800 yard swim; a 12 mile bike ride; and a 3.1 mile run. (You lose *me* at "500 to 800 yard swim.")

- An "Olympic" distance is a 1500 yard swim; a 26 mile bike ride; and a 6.2 mile run. (Ouch!)

- A "Half-Ironman" is a 1.2 mile swim; a 56 mile bike ride; and a 13.2 mile run. (Seriously?)

- A "Full-Ironman" is a 2.4 mile swim, a 112 mile bike ride; and if that's not enough for you, a full 26.2 mile marathon to top it off. (Who *are* these people?)

I know one should never say never, but I'll leave triathlons to Beth, and while she's at it, the single marathons, too.

So how many hours are taken away from family time with the necessary training for any of these? Ultimately, to train properly, her schedule went upside down. She was up at 4:30 AM for swim training at 5:00, then back to help Burt fix the girls breakfast; then on to a carpool run; then five to six hours at work, and carpool again. She ran and biked on the beach with her girls for training each evening. Dinner preparation was next. Then family time again with the girls for homework, and to bed at 9:00 PM. At 4:30 AM the alarm clock rang again. This was the competitor lifestyle. "The early hour was chosen because my swimming buddy and I wanted to make sure we still got to see our families in the mornings."

"You have a goal," she says, "you start step by step, and on days when you feel the stamina isn't there, you do it anyway." Eight months after her swim training, and a year after the "dare" she finally got the courage to do a triathlon. Off she went. She started a "tri" club with other women, and they swam, rode, and ran together as they managed their mother and wife roles. She pursued swim training with dogged determination for six months. Friends and clients stepped up to help her. "We all swam together during the week, one way or another."

The Huntington Beach triathlon was her first. Her age group was written on the back of her legs, as winners are picked from each age group. She was excited, nervous, and ready to go. She backstroked the swim, and during the bicycle ride, watched young competitors fly by.

She struck up a conversation with a woman riding beside her named Kim. It was to be continued at the finish line after Beth arrived before her in the final portion of the competition, the foot race. She watched for Kim to cross the finish line. Beth has never met a stranger, and she was about to forge a lifelong friendship with this new acquaintance.

"The camaraderie at triathlons is easy to build," she says, "as they're relatively small events compared to marathons, with races of say, 3000 competitors versus marathons, with usually 20,000-plus racers."

Beth's name was called for second place in her age group.

Later while personal training, she proudly announced that she finished the triathlon to the gentleman who dared her, and showed him her award. "Okay," he said, "now that you've run a triathlon, you need to do an Ironman."

There were many more triathlons to come and two marathons. The marathons tested her mettle, with blisters and moments of diminished confidence that she'd never cross the finish line, but spirited and enthusiastic nonetheless. She always finished.

Her life became full of training stories, as Beth and her new comrades improved as racers. Some were more seasoned than others, and they pushed Beth to increase her strength, stamina, and time. She joined them for ten and 15-mile bike races up steep hills. "I thought *those* were long, hard rides!" She laughs.

"I'll never forget my first triathlon ocean swim. I had never raced in open ocean, and competitors swam all over me!" In a Hemet, California Sprint Triathlon mountain bike ride, she forgot her water in the hot sun.

A gentleman rode past her halfway through the race and handed her a water bottle. "This man had ridden 400 miles over three days in an Oregon race. I realized that I must get tough as well as fast."

Grueling Training for the Ironman Competition

"Our aspirations are our possibilities." - Samuel Johnson

Along came the 2000 inaugural Ironman California competition, and she and her triathlon and marathon friends volunteered as wetsuit strippers, helping competitors jump on their bicycles after their swims.

Many racers were seasoned Ironman competitors, and along with them were competitors who had competed in Sprints and longer distance triathlons. Beth made instant friends as a volunteer.

She was hooked. She was ready to train and do it. She and a number of her coworkers and fellow racers decided they would enter the next Ironman, the following year. This was the biggest commitment yet.

Beth and her friend Ken signed up to run the 2001 Ironman California competition at the same time, eight months before the race. Thus started the training for one of the toughest physical feats of her life.

"People think that if you're a personal trainer, you're very fit, and it's not a big deal to do this. To master three sports and put them together back to back in a race is not something the American Council on Exercise recommends an average American do. I'm an average person just like anyone else, and training time is 20 to 25 hours of pure cardio per week. It's not easy for anyone!"

Training continued to start in the wee hours of the morning, every morning, with the same commitment Beth had made with her earlier triathlon and marathon events.

With the Ironman, the commitment went up more than a notch to meet the distances and toughness required for each segment of the competition.

"Just imagine," she says, "with a swim and determination, you can do what 2000 other people are doing - essentially in the same "bath tub" - at the same takeoff time. Spectators watch in awe as contenders swim with abandon for over two miles!"

(As someone who doesn't enjoy swimming laps, especially in cold water, I cringe when I think of this particular aspect of the race. But I digress.)

Training time brought together Beth and a partner at 5:00 AM daily to start by swimming in a community pool. She'd swim ten laps each day without stopping for one week, and then increase the laps the next week to perhaps 20.

"I had entered Sprint and Olympic triathlon races, however, I had used back strokes and breast strokes along the way," she says. A dear friend, a retired Physical Education teacher, took her to the next step, teaching her the "reach and pull" of the freestyle stroke. Another taught her how to keep at the stroke with yardage and timed intervals.

"Boy, that water was cold. I had veteran racing friends all around me in the pool who were training for their own races, and I pushed myself as they pushed themselves to meet their own goals."

The cold air enveloped her as she jumped out of the pool, and the shaking started even as she stood in a warm shower. With her hair wet, she ran to teach her first fitness class of the morning,

"My arms were so beat I thought they'd fall off," she says. "Add that to a body still trying to adjust to a 4:30 AM rise and shine."

She would put in a full day of work and then meet her friends to do more training. She practiced riding her bicycle on different terrains, including the beach. Her daughters Brianna and Brooke joined her and rode their bikes on the sand, as well.

The "Brick Layers"

Biking and Running and More Biking and Running

"Always bear in mind that your own resolution to succeed is more important than any other." - Abraham Lincoln

Her training went to a new level during summertime when they began doing "brick layers," a training technique where the different sports are practiced singly and then together, layered one on top of another.

"We started small with one sport and then two at a time, or as many as our training time would let us because of scheduling and family time. Often we found ourselves training solo.

We'd ride at 6:30 every Sunday morning, two, three, and then four to five hours at a time. Veteran triathletes and Ironman racers gave us scheduling advice. Families first! Cardio debt second."

Ah, yes, cardio debt. Beth learned to ride, then to run right afterwards for motor memory. Putting 30 miles in on a bike, and then a six-mile run; 50 miles on a bike and then a six to eight-mile run. Then 70 to 80 miles on the bike and ten to 13-mile runs.

"There were sweat, tears, and sometimes blood during this training, only to go home to clean house, mow the lawn, or cook dinner for the family. I had never been so tired in my life."

I can only imagine. I can remember, too, that she took time for friends. I don't even think she rescheduled more than one time for the girlfriend meet-ups that we had planned.

"I remember the drone of the tires against pavement and making another round on Camp Pendleton," she says. Camp Pendleton, a marine base on the San Clemente/Oceanside border, is an important training location with ups and downs in terrain and diverse types of surfaces.

"I fought the winds going north with my quadriceps burning, trying to get home and done on a second loop of l00 miles."

"My friend Ken became just what I needed to push that bike even more. Yes, he was stronger and faster than I, but patient with me as well." She and her friend forged their way through wind and heat, and the cold in Pulgas Canyon. It turned her fingers, face, and feet numb.

"We climbed hills at 8% and 10% inclines, pushing it at three to four miles per hour. I refused to get off that bike and walk! You never forget your burning lungs and legs. I swear to you, it's harder than giving birth!" Many of her women biking partners wholeheartedly agreed.

She bicycled 3536.38 miles during her training for the coming Ironman.

There was one more thing that Beth learned during this time in her afternoon informal gatherings in her garage with racing buddies, sandwiches and popcorn. She finally learned how to change the tires on a bike.

Running and pushing beyond her self-limitations.

Her runs started with a walk and then a jog. Before long she was doing timed intervals on the track and treadmills at the gym. She got to know every face at 5:30 AM. Next up was outdoor running.

"I was challenged by mud, sand, rocks and wet grass in greenbelts around the city in those wee hours. I ran on anything but pavement. My joints were howling."

But the pain subsided, and she could finally do her 15 to 16 miles without discomfort. It didn't happen overnight, but she increased the size of her shoes, iced her knees, and stretched.

Her running miles before the race tallied up to 1,243.25 miles. She began to triple-brick on Saturdays with buddies.

Her swimming miles totaled tallied up to approximately 152 miles. "Boy was I tired."

"And can *I* eat!"

Ok, apparently there is one thing great, ladies, about strenuous, consistent exercise. Eating! It's allowed and then some! "I'd eat *my* meal, then eat off *Burt's meal*, and then go after the *kids' plates* once they finished."

She binged on peanut butter sandwiches, (Hallelujah, my personal faves!) and burgers. Food, food, food, all you can eat: 3500 to 4000 calories a day. "I lost eight pounds of body fat, but only two pounds of weight, with all of that eating. I never lost muscle." Ironman training, ladies?

One of the most important things that Beth learned was to chart her food and calorie input and output. Bottom line is you must eat, and eat right, or as sportsmen say, "You'll bonk!" In layman's terms, you'll "hit the wall!"

The Mental Game
Two to three weeks before the big race, competitors need to taper their training. It's time to give your body a break, have

a life with family and friends, get your hair done, and get your checkups in. "First, you're anxious, then tired, then WOW. I have time off!"

But mentally it started to settle in. "Oh, no, am I ready to pull this together? Can I do this feat of endurance? Everyone had confidence but me."

I was personally one of those who was emphatic about that confidence. I knew Beth was solid. She was a winner in every way. Still is.

Her talent is enormous, and always has been. She talks about childbirth again. "I remember when I was pregnant, the realization in my third trimester that, "Oh, no! I can't get out of this now! I have to go through it! And yet, the experience of childbirth with its emotions and exhilaration is overwhelmingly amazing."

"Success is nothing more than a few simple disciplines practiced every day." - Jim Rohn

Chapter Two:

Race Days in California and Kona!
Beth's Ironman Events

"Courage is being scared to death, and saddling up anyway." - John Wayne

"You never forget an Ironman race. Everyone has their story about that day." - Beth

California

After eight months of training with Ken, Beth was on her way. It was May 19th, 2001.

The night before the big race, sleep, or rather lack of it, was a common experience. "I slept like a baby the night before, although the clock said it was three hours, if even that. I picked up racing buddies at 4:30 AM to avoid what would be a traffic jam at the Oceanside location of the race near my home in San Clemente."

Coincidentally, *my* older brother, a friend of Beth's as well, also competed in this Ironman. Many competitors state a reason why they are participating. Beth wanted to show her girls that they can be and do anything they want in their future. My brother Jim entered the race for Bob, our sibling who had recently passed away. The tributes among the racers, one after the other, were incredibly touching.

At 5:00 AM, food drop-off and body marking began. "I pumped the tires at the last minute, followed by hugs and back-slapping. My family was up and at-em and positioned at the boat basin to assure their place to watch the incredible start of the race, with 2100 swimmers thrashing through the waves." The vibe of the crowd and the racers was magnetic. "I was nervous at this point, making sure I knew where to strip out of my wetsuit and dress for the bike race. There was a wetsuit stripping "alley" and dressing area. It looked good. She could do this.

"It was time. Ken and I put on our "Orca" swim caps. We were READY." We had 17 hours to complete the race, and we were on it.

The competitors marched down the "alley" to start the race. "I smiled the whole way down to the water. I knew if I did I would see smiles from racers and the crowd around me," Beth notes. There were tips from Ken for the swim. He would be on her left. "We marked our swim caps so we wouldn't lose sight of each other." He would keep the pace and Beth would spot for "holes" in the swimming crowd. I think about drowning as people kick and thrash, all of them looking for holes. Ken and Beth slipped into the 57-degree water along with 2098 others.

The Marines shot a cannon and the race began. Burt and the girls dropped their jaws as the water roared up with the racers swimming as fast as they could out of the starting gate. Surprisingly, the competition was polite, with many "Sorries," and "Excuse mes." Holes were abundant and Beth paced herself stroke for stroke with Ken. There was kicking out there, but fortunately Beth was not a victim. "All I could think about was 'Nobody cut into my dance,' please!"

Ken was able to punch up the pace on the final stretch of the swim and left Beth behind, but not by much. After one hour and 19 minutes of swimming, she ran up the ramp, stripped her wetsuit, and YES! She had beaten her practice time by two minutes. Ken had already jumped on his bike and hit the course.

Volunteers were everywhere and helped Beth dress with helmet and gloves. Beth downed chicken noodle soup for fuel. (Well I'll be darned. Chicken noodle soup, eh?) Her transition to biking took 13 minutes.

"I was cold again, even with the hot soup, but it was out of the tent and onto my bike. A volunteer waited for me with it outside the tent. Wow, they were such an amazing part of the team. I was on my way in a 112-mile bike ride." She would ultimately pass Ken on the second loop. It was a pleasure to ride with such amazing athletes keeping company with each other. "I talked with the others the entire route, even up the hills. It was my back yard and I had lots of people to play with, unlike the solitary training I had undergone." The hard work paid off with her 17.5 mile average in the first loop.

Then mayhem was to come. "I lost all of my tubes and CO_2 cartridge pump and cartridges the first 20 miles out when my bike hit an unfamiliar bump. I passed the bike aid station where a friend was out of tubes. The tire truck with backup tubes and tires was nowhere in sight. My safety net was gone." The wait for the trucks can be an hour or more, and a flat can cost the race.

It was time to fuel herself with a PB&J sandwich she had loaded into her back pocket. "It slipped through my fingers and fell to the ground, squished by fellow racers. So much for lunch!" She was 25 miles out of a 112-mile bike race. "I still had Hammergel flasks and four bottles of Sustained Energy with a few PB pretzels and nuts for salt. I couldn't choke those down and sucked the salt and spit them out. Dang, I craved that peanut butter and jelly sandwich." She stopped twice for bathroom breaks, and I would have, too, admitting that "a girl's gotta do what she's gotta do!"

As Beth entered the next 56-mile stretch, she found it quieter, and started breaking into a group of equal speed and cadence.

It was a group of six men, in major hills, ones that Beth knew well from practicing and practicing the course. They raced down a steep hill with a sudden bend to the left, then slowed, startled, as they passed a fatality. "We had been talking about the labor in childbirth thing again for laughs, with our lungs burning to make it to the top of the second hill." It was an emotionally draining scene with the Medivac rescue team signaling them to bike carefully while they rescued three downed bikers. "Two casualties. One covered fatality on a gurney," says Beth. "We were slowed down to five to ten miles an hour. It shook us terribly."

One member of their group said he couldn't go on. Another wanted to know if it was "for real." "As we left the scene, we all wondered the same thing. Did we know the rider who was killed?" They finished the biking together down a wind tunnel, deep in their own thoughts.

The volunteers awaited them for the 26.2 mile run, the final segment of the competition. They helped the racers dress for it, applied sunscreen, and handed out hats, jackets or other options for helping runners. "I wondered how they knew that we individually were coming to the way station. I found out later that the captain of the volunteer teams has a radio that connects with computer chips they attached to us around our ankles, and others read the numbers attached to our clothing." Beth said.

"As I started the run, I saw Burt and the girls and quickly kissed them all and ran, blowing kisses to everyone including the volunteers and the crowd. This was my day, and I was enjoying it!" Her gut had shut down in the last ten to fifteen miles on the bike, and it was tough to wear her fanny pack so she tossed it and ran on. The bloat in her stomach inhibited her food absorption. All oxygen and blood had gone to her muscles for biking and running, and her gastric region was not absorbing the fuel it needed. But, her racing went on. She talked with other racers, teasing them about her age, and prodding them to keep going with "If an old lady can do this, YOU can do this." She jogged alongside a competitor from Canada. He needed Advil and she needed Tums. A perfect exchange. "He told me he was going to propose to his girlfriend at the finish line. He showed me the rock. A wonderful way to propose." She told him why she was doing the Ironman. "It's for my girls." They got to know each other for two hours and Beth insisted he not go down on one knee. His knees were in pain. He promised he would take Beth's advice and sit with his girlfriend on the ground.

"He kicked it in fast in the last mile, and I didn't want to rain on his parade. His girlfriend said "YES!" "I came in behind the young man with Burt running beside me, which I nixed so as not to be disqualified. My girls caught me at the finish line. What a feeling. No one can ever take this away from me. To finish an Ironman! It took me 12 hours, 41 minutes. Yes!"

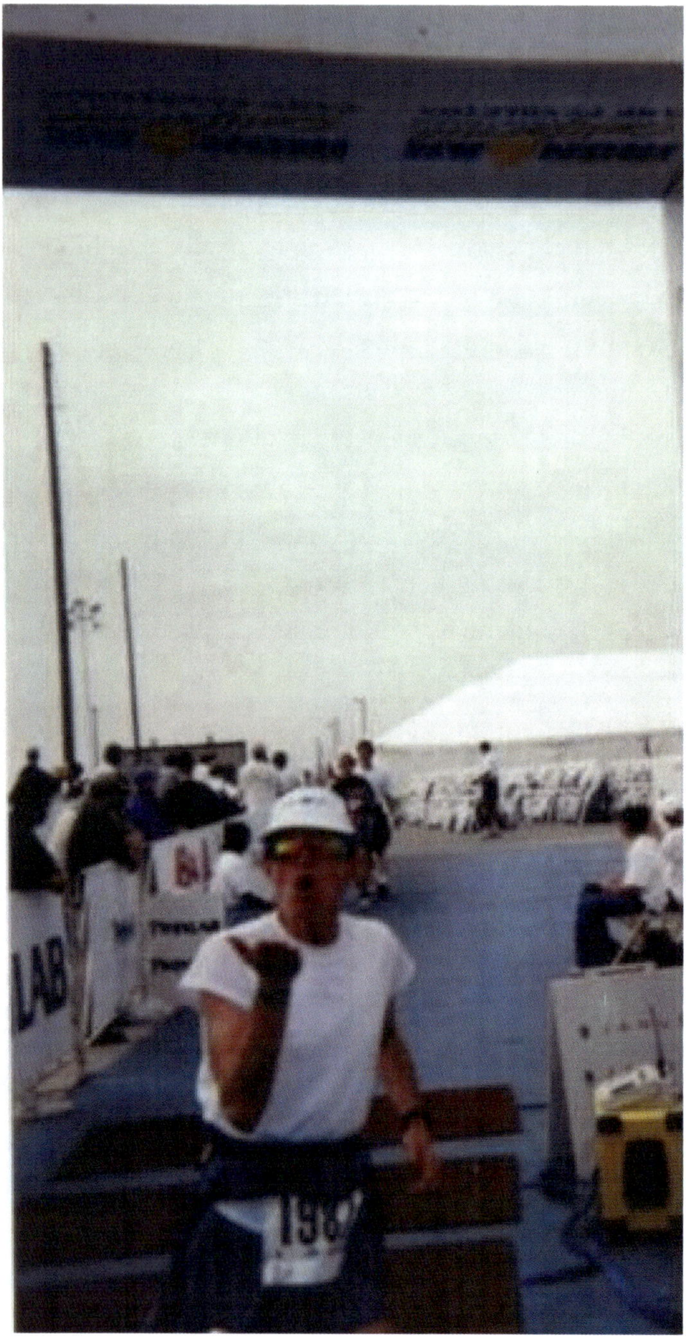
LAB

Beth walked around with her family until she showered. She felt great and then it happened. Her head felt light, she lost hearing, and had spots before her eyes. "Burt picked me up and took me to the MASH tent. It was hypothermia. I was fed chicken soup with my feet up. Burt scooped me up again for the ride home. My only regret was not seeing my buddies crossing the finish line, but they did. We all did it!"

That night she laid in bed with her family, talking with friends and checking the computer for news about the others finishing, and at what times. "I was totally elated," she says.

My own brother finished at 12 hours, 44 minutes, right behind Beth. He experienced the same thing.

Her friend Kim told Beth she had come in third in her age category and needed to be at the breakfast ceremony the next morning. "The awards were announced and what a feeling it was to walk up on that stage for that trophy!" she says. Then came news that 100 competitors out of 2100 earned slots to race in Kona, Hawaii to compete in the most famous and coveted Ironman on earth. Beth was among them. "It was the invitation of a lifetime, from a first try at an Ironman!" The top racers in their age categories from all over the world were qualifiers. The race date was October 6, 2001. Beth would be there.

But Beth had a hurdle. With all of the hours of training, her husband was concerned about her family, and how they never saw her on weekends until 8:00 at night. It was her family or her training. She wanted the Kona Ironman. It was a dream and she loved the competition she'd had. He proposed a deal. She could race Kona as her last Ironman competition.

Another surprise awaited Beth. Two weeks after her California Ironman she competed in the "Rock 'n Roll" San Diego Marathon in June 2001. She qualified for the Boston Marathon.

Kona

Whatever you can do or dream you can, begin it; boldness has genius, power and magic in it. - Goethe

Imagine the Ironman 2.4-mile swim, 112-mile bike ride, and 26.2-mile marathon piled on temperatures of 100 degrees and 50 mile-per-hour winds. Beth took it all in, ready for the challenge. It was NOT for the weak. In this race, even blood tests were administered for each athlete to look at how endurance athletes are affected by extreme racing.

Burt and the girls had accompanied her and would join her at the finish line as they cheered her on.

She floated with 2500 racers bobbing in the ocean, waiting for the starting signal. "At 7:00 AM, it's a go, and it's every man and woman for themselves." Beth says. Competitors swim with abandon through the waves for over two miles. Once again, it's a jaw dropping scene for spectators.

Beth found the shore and dashed to a quick shower to wash off the salt. It was fast. Her bicycle awaited her for the next segment of the Ironman, the 112-mile bike race. She was equipped with food and electrolytes. Bathrooms were located along the route with stopping points for resting.

She jumped on her bike and rode with fervor. Suddenly, she was riding on lava with heavy winds battering her. A tire goes flat at 33 miles out. She has carried two tubes with her, and hurriedly fixes it. She punches it to make up for time.

Then, bam. A second flat at 49 miles. She jumped off to switch it out. She turned around at Havi, and another blew at 52 miles. The "flat" truck came by and fixed it. The truck stayed with her and, sure enough, there was to be a fourth flat at 80 miles out. They fixed it and she was on her way.

Could she make it to the finish line within the time limit, considering the lost time? She knew there were only a few hours left. The fierce competitor within her broke out. She put her bike in the tents and ran at full speed, intent on finishing within the time limit, even with flats and 100 degrees bearing down on her.

Her children jumped the fence to run into the finish line. Leis were everywhere.

"Kona is tough. It's a world championship and every year it's stifling hot, with the wind and the lava rock." Beth explains.

Would she do it again if she could? Oh yes. "Kona's the one that challenges your abilities. The first time is just the hazing, and then there's the desire to go back and do it as a veteran who knows what to expect. You're hooked on it once you do it. You'll want to come back again and again to finally conquer its severity and feel that rush."

From then on, she acted as a coach to Ironman contestants, and picked up once again on bicycling with the girls and Burt beside her. It was family time once again.

"What we once enjoyed, we can never lose. All that we love deeply becomes a part of us." - Helen Keller

Chapter Three:

THE ACCIDENT THAT SHATTERED HER SPINE AND HER WORLD

After her exciting races, Beth continued to enter racing competitions. She and Burt had decided to enter the "Guacamole Grande," a 50-mile biking competition through the hills of Temecula, California. It was a race that would change her life in unimaginable ways. As Beth flew ahead of her competitors, riding alone, her bicycle skidded through wet broken asphalt, flying out from underneath her. She was slammed onto her back, knocked out cold.

When Beth opened her eyes after the accident, still on the ground, the face of a friend, a fireman who was also competing in the race, was at her head, looking at her, "Beth, stay still." At her feet was an orthopedic surgeon, a competitor who came upon the scene. The fireman said to her, "You may have a spinal cord or brain injury. Just stay still."

She felt nothing as the ambulance arrived, just an irritation in her back, as if she was lying on an uneven surface. She was loaded onto a gurney and placed into the ambulance where, in route to the hospital, a medical box fell on her chest and broke four ribs. She went unconscious again, and woke up in the emergency room under a CAT scan. Even then she felt no pain. But this would change dramatically. She had shattered the T6-7 vertebrae like glass and stabbed her spinal cord, which then leaked spinal fluid.

At the hospital, miraculously, a neurosurgeon was there for another surgery, but they rushed Beth into the operating room. She remembers hearing her husband Burt at her side. "You're going to be okay. We'll take care of you."

Eight hours of surgery later, she awoke, sobbing with confusion in Intensive Care. "I was put back together like Humpty Dumpty, with a bone graft from my hip and rods and screws." She could barely hear her husband's voice. She slipped back into sleep.

The next day she opened her eyes. Burt and her mother were next to her. The neurosurgeon arrived and described what she had been through, the surgery, and the results. It was then she was told she was a paraplegic and would never walk again. She was going to be in a wheelchair for the rest of her life. Burt immediately assured her, over and over, "Beth, I am committed to you. I am committed to you." Her head spun, taking it all in.

Coming up were months of hospitals, a body cast, going home to her children in a wheelchair, another surgery by a specialist in Colorado, and more months of limited movement.

Imagine being Beth right after her accident. Imagine needing to learn how to slide from a wheelchair into a bed and back. Imagine having to figure out how to use the bathroom facilities. How to dress yourself. How to move in a "chair," as wheelchairs are often referred to by disabled individuals. Imagine having to figure out how to slide in and out of a vehicle.

Imagine being in almost unbearable pain, unable to move, or to do the simplest things. Imagine having a mind going over and over the trauma, your head spinning with confusion and uncertainty about who you are, who you'll be, and what you'll be.

Imagine your first trip out in public in your chair on a sidewalk, or parked in a handicapped space and drawing attention from passersby. To be someone whom strangers will always look right past, or as Beth says, "Right over your head," not wanting to make eye contact. Perhaps because they fear that your condition could happen to them?

I can't imagine how it must have been for Beth to try to envision her life unfolding as she lay in her hospital bed. Can you? That horrible experience of the accident was shocking, disorienting, and devastating for Beth and her family.

Yet, with their faith, one day at a time, Beth and her family got a little stronger and more focused. Clarity was coming bit by bit. Each day brought tiny improvements in physical and mental strength.

Imagine when perhaps the realization sets in - maybe, just maybe, life can go on. Perhaps you'll move forward into your life's "new normal," a life with disappointments, discouragements, and detours. A life unplanned, but a new life that goes into the future nonetheless. Who will you be? What purpose awaits you? Can you ever find joy again?

The Start of Excruciating Chronic Pain

Many of us think that paralysis is only a condition of lack of movement ability, and limbs that are numb to being touched, and are unable to feel any outside stimuli. This is only partly true. It's a misconception, probably accepted because we able-bodied rarely get to know someone who has a spinal cord injury and paralysis.

The truth is, an injured spinal cord brings tremendous pain. It is overwhelmingly hard to overcome. It is a pain that will stay with you as long as you live.

While Beth was in intensive care, her pain did not start in the first few days. She had no idea what was coming. One night, in her hospital bed, she awoke with searing, white-hot pain, worse than any pain she had ever experienced, including during childbirth.

She attempted to press the nursing station button to get immediate help, but it was out of reach. No one heard or saw her. In the morning, her mother arrived and immediately knew that Beth was in agony. White as a sheet and sweating, writhing in the bed. Her mother bolted to the nurse's station and, in no uncertain terms, told them to get into her daughter's room. This was the start of a pain that Beth had to learn how to live with.

After Beth's surgery and onset of pain, she was transferred from her first hospital to a spinal cord rehabilitation hospital, St. Jude's in Fullerton, California. She spent three months there, learning how to "live" in a Kydex body cast that kept her back straight. She struggled through pain to learn how to pull herself out of bed, and how to slide into a wheel chair. She relearned how to go in and out of cars with atrophied legs. She re-learned how to control her bladder and bowels. She was discharged in her body cast and wheelchair. Her husband repeated that he was dedicated to her, and committed to her care and their relationship.

Chapter Four:

Bouncing Back and Resurrecting Her Dream

Beth arrived at her home after six months of hospitalization and rehabilitation. Her home was ready for her. Burt had prepared the household to meet her wheelchair needs for her homecoming, including reconstructing a ground-level bathroom. Her mother helped with homemaking. Burt had managed the girls' lives with carpooling and school, in addition to bringing them to see Beth once a week in the hospital. He had moved a bed down into the family room, near her bathroom, and much to Beth's delight, the girls decided to "camp out" with her, and join her in sleeping in the family room as well. "This lasted through the summer," Beth says. "The Sanden family campout was just another part of my family's new normal."

The first time we wobbled on a bicycle we became acutely aware of the prospects of suffering physical pain. It served to make us more tentative because we appreciated the risk involved. But the joy of learning to ride was stronger than the fear of danger, so we practiced the skills necessary until the fear was overcome with joy. - Leo Buscaglia

Her homecoming was frightening, as she wondered how she could be a good wife and mother to her two girls. "How was I going to raise two teenagers?" Even the simplist things were difficult. She was unable to use stairs, for instance, and the girls' rooms were on the second floor.

"The first 'mom' thing I had to do happened one week after my return. My oldest was verbally disrespectful to me, and I was not going to let it go. I rolled my chair up to the stairs, still in my body cast, and slowly but surely climbed out of the chair and onto the stairs. I hoisted one leg after the other, and made it to the first platform. I managed to keep going up the next set. It took me 20 minutes to climb those stairs on my south end."

She reached her daughter's bedroom door, and on the floor, knocked. When her daughter appeared, Beth told her, "I am STILL your mother, and I'm not done talking to you yet." Through her unimaginable pain and restricted motion, she demonstrated her resolve to get back into life. We can only imagine the tone of her voice.

Soon, she was told about a spinal surgeon in Colorado who had a surgical procedure that removed the rods and screws from damaged spines, replacing the hardware with a different material. It was resulting in significantly lessened pain levels.

The trip was planned. Fourteen months after the accident, Beth underwent the surgery and returned home. I remember visiting her afterwards. She was on the floor on a large pillow. She wasn't allowed to move for several weeks, and still in pain, she wanted to be in the family room. As I sat down with her, she pulled out a large baggie of literally what looked like construction size hardware. She truly did have large rods and screws holding together her spine. It was shocking.

Unfortunately, Beth's pain did not subside from the surgery, and the doctor's prognosis was the same: she would never walk again.

But wait. Let's meet her *now*.

The first thing you notice about Beth when you meet her is her phenomenal smile, the biggest and brightest you have ever seen. It illuminates every room. Her smile has radiated around the world, and her joy with racing once again, this time as a disabled competitor, and connecting with everyone she meets, never dims. With well over a year of physical therapy and swimming, she painstakingly regained partial use of one leg. She graduated from a chair to a walker, and then a walker to a cane.

Beth traveled back to Colorado to see the surgeon who had attempted to help her. She walked into his office with the help of a walker, swinging her still paralyzed leg, and steadying herself with her rehabilitated leg. To his surprise, it was the first time he had ever seen anyone with her type of spinal cord injury stand up from a wheelchair and walk.

Her life began to change. "My ability to race after my paralysis was something that I attribute to God," says Beth. "How could there be any other source of the speed and strength I've been given? How else did I keep going, after getting the devastating news about my paralysis? How else did I brave 90 degrees in the Great Wall of China marathon? How else did I cycle across the moonscape of Antarctica, or race in the deadly cold of the Arctic?

"I say, 'thank you, God' for the use of one leg. I get to drive because my working leg is the gas and brake pedal leg. I was so excited about that! I have a new purpose in life: to be authentic and give others joy."

"There's a saying, *Sometimes God lets you hit rock bottom so that you will discover that He is the rock at the bottom.*' This is exactly what happened to me, and I made it off the bottom to a place of joy at the top. My life is a miracle."

You, too, might have your own metaphorical rock bottom and the inspiration of a different faith. Beth shows us that you can climb up and regain your footing.

70

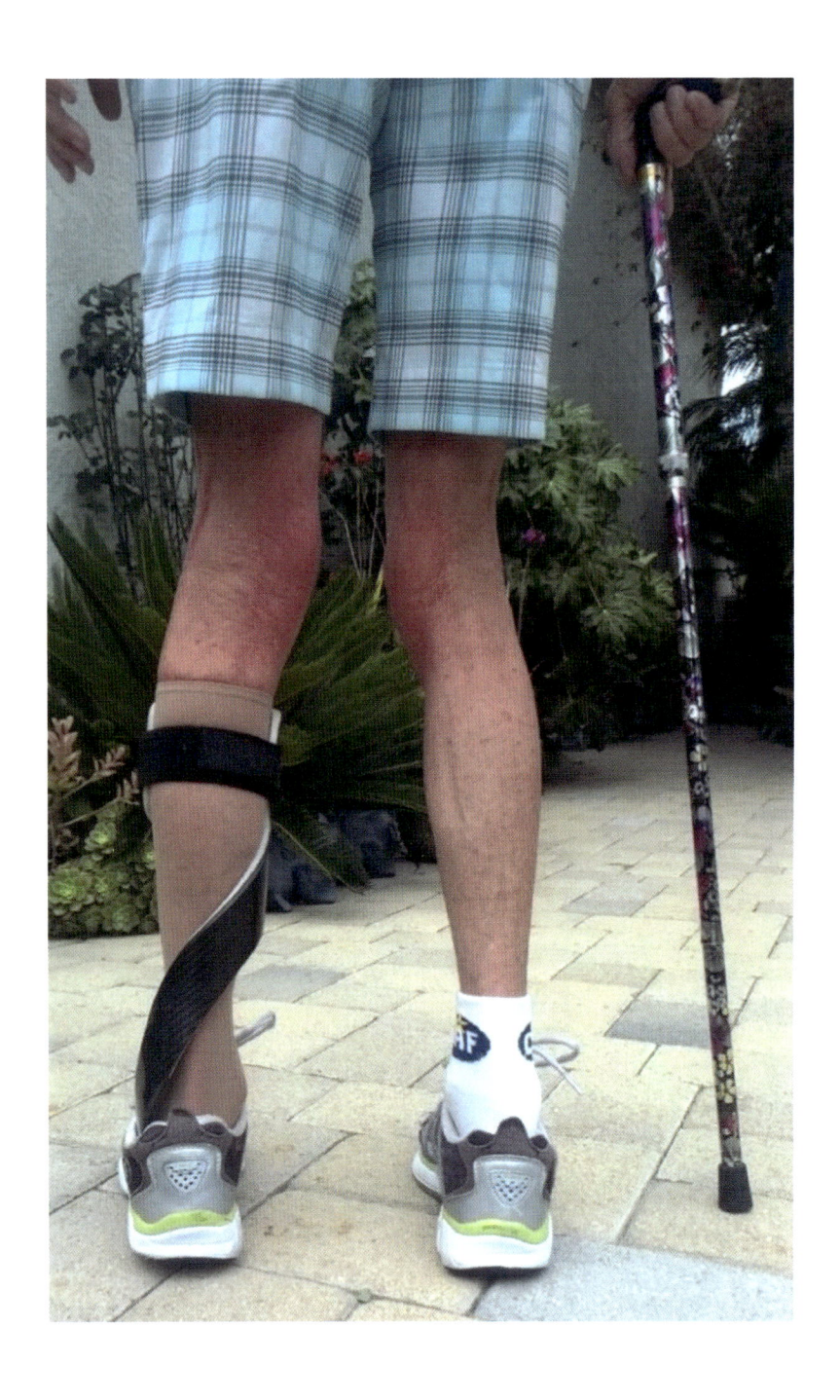

A Rock Bottom Story

I remember going through the death of my 23-year-old brother at 17. He had suffered from schizophrenia for three years during a time when shock treatment was the only option he had for therapy. His condition was devastating for all of us siblings and indescribably tragic for my parents. I remember my father breaking down in tears one day when he and I were alone together. He had just found out that the only "next option" was to "commit" my brother. It was a lot for a 17-year-old to take in. I spent half of my teenage years visiting my highly medicated brother, whom I dearly loved, in hospitals for the mentally ill. At that time, everyone described them as "nut houses," including my friends. They didn't know any better. However, I was quick to tell them that, yes, and my brother was in lockdown in every one of them at some point in time.

I wish I could say my experience of tragedy and loss at such a young age would be my last until I was a ripe old age. But it wasn't to be. At 43, I lost my father to Alzheimer's, and at 45 I lost another brother and my mother, ten weeks apart. I could only imagine the endless tears of my mother after losing two sons. It was too much. My family of seven was now three: another brother, my sister, and me.

Benched on the Sidelines of Life

I was essentially "benched," unable to navigate the detour that was thrown into my journey in life. I functioned with my writing and inspirational gift businesses. I marched on, doing radio, going to business meetings, yes, but my speaking career was over. I couldn't come to life in front of an audience. I no longer knew who I was. I missed the "me" I had been, but I wasn't strong enough to bring her back again. I had hit rock bottom.

Beth was there. Her faith was so strong, she was able to remind me of mine. Hers spilled over onto me.

The "New Normal"

Her husband Burt coined the "new normal" slogan. Beth took the motto and applied it to those of us whose lives have taken a difficult, unexpected turn, a loss, an interruption like an obligation to care-taking, a business failure, a war that injures us, anything that disrupts our goals and dreams, throws us a left hook, and sends us into a detour. She had to find her "new normal" after the accident changed everything in her life.

"We all have to find a new normal for ourselves. It's there inside you. You'll find it," she says. "It doesn't always come quickly, but if you want to go forward in life again, you need to look for it. It's where you're supposed to be." She explains that not everyone makes it to their new normal. They cannot move on, and many quit halfway and don't make it out of "where they are." Sadly, others don't make it at all.

It took me a very long time to embrace my new normal, to realize I could reignite my journey to my future. What I learned from Beth was that it's not the end of your life ahead of you.

You can still be the *more* that you always hoped to be. You can still find empowerment and ways to contribute to the world, like you were always meant to do. You can rev up the engine of your talents again and go full speed.

Beth sat at my side throughout my search for a new normal. She kept me focused by using my talents, and we brainstormed the writing she needed for her athletic coaching, personal training, and fitness business. She gave me emotionally rewarding work and time with me processing my challenges.

I watched *her* overcome her pain and disability, and achieve a point where she accepted her new body, and celebrated how blessed she was with one working leg. It gave her great joy through pain and through her disability. Others in wheelchairs are not so lucky. It's very tough for them to reach a new normal, and we able-bodied are not immune to an agonizing process as well.

"The measure of a life, after all, is not its duration, but its donation." - Corrie Ten Boom

"I love my body because it's what God gave me to reach out to everyone. My accident taught me that I'm now a tool to use to help others!" Beth believes.

From here, Beth went on to her first Boston Marathon to race the race that was waiting for her before the accident. She would go on to race three more. In her first, as with all of them, as she cycled on her handcycle that allowed her arms to power her through, she stopped and blew kisses to the crowds, joyous that she had finally achieved a goal that had been sidelined for four years.

Chapter Five:

Do you long to resurrect a dream?

Or start over again and create another?

"Always remember the future comes one day at a time." - Dean Acheson

Perhaps in your own life you have a dream, or maybe more than one, that has kept you hoping for your future, and participating actively in life, but has been sidelined or even abandoned due to life's many distracting and difficult detours. You might have lost your job. Maybe you were diagnosed with a challenging health condition that is life-changing, and you have hard decisions to make.

Perhaps you've lost a loved one, or are in an exhausting caretaker role for one. You might have had an accident that has damaged your ability to function physically like able-bodied people.

You might have been a soldier wounded in war. Or, you're feeling terribly lonely and isolated. These are just a few of life's unexpected twists and turns, many of which can be unbearable, and seem to be impossible to overcome.

Please remember, you are not alone. Most of us, at some time or another, wonder if our dreams will ever be achieved. This is true for many of us, just as it was for Beth as she embarked on the journey to becoming a champion able-bodied racer. Her accident turned her life and her racing upside down. In the aftermath, with months and months of pain, rehabilitative therapies, surgeries, and trying to discover and define her "new normal," Beth knew her future as a physically disabled person was uncertain. In her darkest moments, she may have struggled to even picture another dream, or another purpose. She may have grieved over what she believed was a dream lost.

The idea that we must abandon a dream can lead to deep sadness, a loss of hope for the future, or the loss of wonderment about life. All of a sudden you feel like you can't define yourself or the road ahead for you, or whether you'll ever have another dream.

But you know what? You will. Whether you'll resurrect the elusive one you are discouraged about right now, or dare to dream another, you can be back believing in one again. Have faith that you will.

Sometimes, as in Beth's case before her accident, she had to begin a grueling period of extreme activities to even hope of capturing her dream of competition in races. She honestly didn't know if she could do it. But, every day, she found exhilaration in getting out there in the water, getting on her bicycle, and running as fast as she could, one day at a time. There were days when she wanted to throw in the towel, but she kept the alarm set for 4:30 AM and did it again. Every day, things changed. Every day, she conquered another mile, a farther swim, and a better time on the stop watch.

I believe that dreams are tied intricately to the purpose we see for our lives. Consider when you were a young child, and you had a dream about your future, easily answering "What I want to be when I grow up." You knew your purpose in a child's way. I guarantee that most young children are pretty clear about what they love to do, what they see as their future, and how they want to live and be as people. Do they want to make music and entertain others? Do they want to help people? Do they like drawing comics, or getting under the hood of a car, or pretending to be our president?

Ask them. Talking about this lights them up and animates them. Lest we think they're foolish, (don't kid yourself, you know a lot of parents do), doesn't it remind you of the dreams and sense of purpose you had then? What were those?

I know several people who followed the dreams of their childhood. Two examples were classmates in high school. One started drawing in his early years and dreamt he would be an artist. He continued to draw throughout school and into college. Where did that dream take him? How did he use his sense of purpose?

He bought a famous older syndicated comic strip and revived it. Then he created another syndicated comic strip about teenagers and their habits. This continues to amuse fans to this day. And all because he loved to draw. He knew as a child it was his dream and his purpose.

The other was a young man who was drawn to science all of his childhood. He figured out that if he became a doctor he could use this fascination for good. At our 20th high school reunion he told me he was an anesthesiologist in San Francisco. He knew early in his life that he had a dream and a purpose.

I know of other stories of individuals who, in their elementary school years, knew what they were meant to do. Another former alumnus loved playing with makeup as a child and created her own "formulas" and mixtures to proudly show off to her parents. Guess what she did as an adult? Yes, making makeup was her dream and helping women become beautiful inside and out with a strong self-esteem became her purpose. She started a makeup line and today she flies in her own private jet.

I truly believe that revisiting our childhoods can be an illuminating process for recovering the dreams deep within us, and our sense of purpose. We're all different, but I promise you will find yours again, if you will honestly think back to yourself as a child, and just be an observer of your "then" self. Do it in a nonjudgmental way. See who you really are and what you believed you could be and do.

Is it possible that your sense of purpose and dreams could have morphed into something else since your childhood? Of course. But who you were as a youngster and how you evolved until now are uniquely you.

I once wrote resumes for a living and one day interviewed a college student to craft a resume from a medical slant to something she could use to pursue a new career. She had a wonderful story about how she was altering her dream from becoming a doctor to something else rather surprising. She told me her story. She was in college studying the sciences and chose an internship in the Pacific Northwest to study habits of whales.

On a boat day in and day out, she observed their lives. She saw their amazingly close communities, how mothers tended their calves, and their emotions. Once the whales had gotten to know her, they regularly visited her at the side of her boat, to interact with her and show their affection through touch.

She dropped a bombshell on her parents. Her sense of purpose to help others who need her hadn't changed, because she could help the whales with their lives. But her dream did.

"I knew after spending time with the whales, watching their lives unfold, I had to be with them. I have to be with the whales," she told me.

"The shoe that fits one person pinches another; there is no recipe for living that suits all cases." - Carl Jung

My beliefs about a child's "knowing" who they are and what their dreams and sense of purpose might be come from a vivid personal experience. My mother was an English teacher for many years, as well as a Russian history and literature teacher. I remember as a child, going through my mother's books at home. None of them were romance novels, although there's nothing wrong with that, but all we had in our home to read, aside from the ubiquitous encyclopedia set of the times, were books by Russian authors; the classics, both American and English; poetry of all types; and English grammar and composition books.

So, from the time I was in Kindergarten, I was reading American, English and Russian literature, as well as the daily comic strips. I was a child, after all! An interesting foreshadowing of my future happened when I was eight or nine. I started cutting out "Peanuts" comic strips and replacing the dialog bubbles above the characters with my own conversations. I even made a book out of construction paper with a yarn binding, telling a whole new story with the characters by cutting them out and placing them in position on the pages.

Then in high school, when we students were offered to pick either an essay test, or a multiple- choice test in most classes, I always picked the essay. This was true during my entire education.

Finally, as I entered the corporate world, it was because of my writing. In order to become a Training Specialist at the Zale Corporation, I passed a verbal interview and clinched the job with a mandatory essay. The position required about 80% composition, and fulfilled my dream of writing professionally and my purpose of helping people to improve their working lives.

Fulfillment of dreams is tied to happiness, is it not? Must your dreams be so lofty as those I mention above? No, they just must be true for you, no matter what they are. If you're feeling helpless now because you believe you've lost your sense of purpose and the dreams that created it, you realize that it's why we suffer inside so badly when we have disappointments, discouragements, and detours.

But wait. Don't give up. Beth didn't give up, and I'm sure the folks I mention above had deflating setbacks along their journey as well. I'm sure they had to adjust to a new normal at some point in their lives. It's possible they had moments of despair, or of feeling overwhelmed with confusion, or feeling like a failure. It's all part of the human experience.

I remember, at 33, it was my turn to feel like I might give up. My adult life had always been like a whirling dervish. I would drop everything and travel to Paris on a dime. I would drive to Los Angeles airport and hop a plane to Mexico City to go dancing. Yes, there was a time when you could do that! It was great! I'd also jump in my car on a whim and drive cross-country by myself.

I blew through two marriages, and moved all over the states to take new jobs or work on contract. Through it all I never, ever slept through the night. I couldn't be still with myself. My brain was on overdrive constantly. The travel and the moves were about trying to run away from my own head, which was constantly spinning with an overload of energy. I'd dance all night to blow it out.

Then it happened. I had a psychological breakdown at 33 years-old. My sister knew it was happening. One of my moves had been to California, where I was once again close to family. I could not afford insurance at the time, but she helped me find a free brain disorder research clinic. I think it saved my life. I have continued under doctors' care. I now sleep at night and am very happy with my home in Georgia, where I have found a peace in my beautiful wooded surroundings. I no longer feel the need to run away from my own head.

"When we were children, we used to think that when we were grown up we would no longer be vulnerable. But to grow up is to accept vulnerability...to be alive is to be vulnerable."

- Madeleine L'Engle

My hope is that these few suggestions below will help you live after, or with, any condition that has you reeling with an uncertain future. Perhaps they will help breathe inspiration back into your life, and set you on a path to resurrecting your dreams and purpose.

So how can we step back into the journey of resurrecting dreams, or creating new ones?

"Trust yourself. You know more than you think you do." - Benjamin Spock

Let's dive into some things that could help you climb back on the path to your dreams and sense of purpose.

Harness the power of self-acceptance "where you are."

So, who are you? Funny how, in our culture, people answer that question with *what they do*, as opposed to who they are. I do it. You probably do, too. Why is it that way? I mean, if you say "I'm a banker," what happens if you lose your job and are having a difficult time finding another? Then who are you?

Self-acceptance in the here and now will help you persevere in your circumstances. Be who you are intended to be. Have faith that you can once again be yourself and break through your disappointments, discouragement and detours.

Knowing who you are at your core, and being comfortable in your own skin goes a long way to helping you resurrect a dream and overcome your discouragements, disappointments and detours.

Who you are is a belief that you can carry with you into all of life's ups and downs. Being genuinely yourself and describing your life as a woman or man on a mission, helps you to visualize yourself in the future.

Break the habit of self-criticism and trying to be what others are. Accept yourself where you are and hold on to that. It's yours. You never need to feel "less than."

Visualize walking forward, embracing who you are now. Be confident that you have, or will have, a dream because you are someone who wants one. Wanting one is a powerful statement. Let it fly. Give it wings.

Create a spark of fascination.

"Look at everything as though you were seeing it for the first time... Then your time on earth will be filled with glory." -
Betty Smith

Your journey through disappointments, discouragements, detours, or disabilities, does not mean you are "unabled." Yes, it's so hard to be able to see past your day-to-day challenges if you are in circumstances that seem beyond your control, and impossible to navigate.

The idea of fascination, however, gives you a chance to see things in a new light, no matter how big or small, or how insignificant they might be. See your current disappointment, discouragement, or detour with fascination and curiosity as a source of learning and a path to growth.

See the details of your life in the here-and-now, view them with curiosity, and see them in ways you may not have before. Curiosity was something encouraged during childhood, but faded as we became adults. It is often considered unessential as a grownup, when an appearance of authoritativeness becomes important.

But if we lose our curiosity, we can also lose our energy, our ability to be surprised or spontaneous, and our interest in pursuing new things. We can also lose our interest in resurrecting a dream, leaving us confused about how to move forward mentally, or physically, emotionally, or all the above.

A new perspective of curiosity can help you start the path to a resurrected or new sense of purpose and a dream, with great enjoyment because you are not limited in what your dream can be.

You can hold that dream dear with a fascination that can enrich your life right where you are, right now.

> *"The mind is not a vessel to be filled, but a fire to be rekindled."* - Plutarch

Visualize your future.

If you are trying to "find your way back" to your former self in your current situation, consider turning that around and instead of looking back, look forward and create a new vision for yourself. You are probably in a state that we call a "new normal." That new normal holds promise for the resurrection of your dreams and purpose with some adjustments for moving forward.

One way to look toward your future is to read books and magazines that you enjoy and strike you as excellent sources for helping you to visualize the life you'd love to pursue. Look at pictures in magazines, read books, listen to podcasts, and take courses that universities offer online for free. Find a joy in these. They're just for you.

Then take action. If you love prayer, pray. If you love meditation, be still. If you love church fellowship, go; or fellowship at your synagogue, or other place of worship. If you love book clubs, dive into the experience of losing yourself in a good read. If you love yoga, go and enjoy the challenge of the poses, and the camaraderie.

Do anything, no matter how minuscule it seems. Sometimes that's all we can do. But each small action accomplished, added to another small action, and another small action, and so forth, adds up to something bigger; a bigger permission to be who you are at the moment, to read and visualize, to find more ways to create a snippet of joy, and to have an expanded belief in your potential.

All of these can inspire you to visualize a life that can someday crystalize for you.

Cast off your self-limiting beliefs.

Unfortunately, somehow between childhood and becoming adults, many of us put on the brakes with our dreams. We're convinced by societal directives to work at something deemed "valuable," like accounting, law, and yes, medicine, as my friend did above, and also, management in most of those careers. I'm just sayin'.

We're encouraged to look for corporate jobs and great health insurance. It's what I did. Certainly, those are awesome options for forging a path toward a dream. They often bring security and a lucrative future.

But here's the thing. We're not all cut out for that. There's certainly no dearth of other career paths. Beth followed a path as a personal trainer and coach, something she loves to do, and finds nourishing for her purpose to help people. And, by the way, her university training was in nursing. She did indeed follow the medical path, but realized that her heart was in the fitness industry.

It's easy for us to become limited by beliefs that stomp on our self-esteem and tell us we're too old, or too disabled, too unintelligent, too depressed, or too unattractive to dream. Don't believe it! Take those limiting beliefs, and tell them to get lost. Replace them with mental and physical pictures of something that you'd love to do.

Keep them in your mind and anytime you want the sensation of being unlimited, observe them and enjoy. It's your personal dream and path. Let no one try to squash it.

The stories above of incredible success by giving their childhood dreams a nod and a "Yes!" with commitment to a dream and purpose at all costs are not meant to discourage you or make you feel "less than."

We all have our own path, and your success is defined in your own way. These stories illustrate how you can overcome your negative self-talk that tells you that you cannot reach your dreams.

Replace negative self-imposed limits with a belief in yourself and how you can resurrect dreams and a sense of purpose.

Tell yourself that these pesky limitations are there, embedded in your brain, and figure out why. I think most of us have an idea if we dig deep! Then punt them like a football, or slam them with a tennis racket, or throw them like a rock into the ocean.

There. Much better. Now, get back to who you are, and dream.

Like Beth, my sister-in-law was a champion racer well into her adult years. She achieved a Guinness World Record. She was a school teacher five days a week who ran every day before, and after leaving, her elementary school classroom.

We were looking through her memorabilia this summer, and I was in awe at the amount of news press she received as a groundbreaking runner for women. She ran and ran and ran, becoming a weekend marathon contender against men, and an ultra-marathoner, running over 100 miles in individual races.

She said that with every race, her love of running took over at the starting line. She was ready and chomping at the bit.

Self-limitations were not allowed. Her desire to cross the finish line kicked in and never left her mind. She pictured it over and over and over. She knew she would cross that finish line in every race, and place as well. She did.

She retired from teaching, and like Beth, she continues to run and run, and also started a personal training business to help clients achieve better health. She is still going strong, training clients six days a week. Her age number, beyond Beth's, need not apply.

See yourself as a work in progress.

"The privilege of a lifetime is being who you are." - Joseph Campbell

Sounds impossible when you're struggling, or in pain, or exhausted, or lonely, doesn't it? Actually, this is something that can be a way to move yourself into a more fulfilling future. It's a project with no end date. It's not supposed to have one.

Continue all of your life to evolve as a work in progress and find satisfaction in personal transformation. This needn't be a fast process, even a snail's pace is fine. One step at a time, my friends, one step at a time.

In fact, being a work in progress takes practice. Pick a goal for yourself in your current situation. Can you become more attentive to a dream inside you? What's a perfect small step to keep it alive?

Are you shaping a personal purpose that gives you great satisfaction in the here and now? Are you forging or deepening relationships with those around you?

Can you practice being *more of who you are*, and *more of what you'd like to be,* even within the constraints you have around you?

There's never a better time than now to commit to being a work in progress. Studies show that those who consider themselves a work in progress are among the most happy. They're people just like you and me. They're living lives just like ours. They've made a determined commitment to being better selves in a variety of ways, lofty or otherwise, every day. You choose the path to personal progress that's all about you.

Writing this book has been a dream I've held for many years, as I've said. My purpose with my skill for finding just the right words to help others has guided me through decades of writing and speaking.

I hoped that Beth would choose me to tackle this, as I knew she had so many wonderful friends and contacts from her racing over the last several years. Any one of them could be qualified to do this. I accepted that, but had my heart set on it.

After many, many years of friendship and working on writing and instructional projects together, it was, and still is in writing this, a dream I've held dear.

Then one day, the "door opened." Beth emailed me, "Diane, I'm ready to write the book." I asked if she was certain that she wanted me to write it, and I assured her that if she had someone else in mind, I understood.

In essence, she said, "No, I want you."

I picked up my dream, dusted it off, and took the leap I had wanted to take for a long time. You can do it, too.

Advance confidently in the direction of your dreams, and endeavor to live the life you imagine. You will meet with a success unexpected in common hours.

- Henry David Thoreau

Chapter Six:
Triumphant on the Great Wall of China

Beth's kisses at the Boston Marathon did not go unnoticed by a certain diplomat from China. His outreach to her would change her life. She had qualified to be one of eight handcyclists in the 2010 Boston Marathon, and was subsequently invited to the Great Wall of China Marathon.

This gentleman went back to his country and asked the government organizers of the Great Wall of China Marathon if they would allow Beth to participate. They would. They accepted and helped financially, along with the Challenged Athletes Foundation (CAF), to pay Beth's way, with her husband's accompaniment, including plane tickets and hotel.

Race day was May 1, 2011. Using a walker, a leg strap, a cane, and handcycle to finish on the road at the end of the race, she completed it in 7 hours and 20 minutes, finishing within the time limit for the abled-bodied racers. She was the first challenged athlete to do so.

The Great Wall of China contains 20,518 steps, with loose stones and gravel, missing steps, some steps one to three feet in height, broken and unleveled, along with crumbling walls.

Beth forged through brutal temperatures and a 14-mile uneven surface of the Wall, with its rocky foot path, and irregular staircases. Burt followed behind, and assisted her when she would tumble down them, making sure she didn't hit the actual Wall itself. I viewed one video of her in the race, falling forward off of a staircase, onto the stones, and it brought me to tears. But not *her*. She popped up and flashed her incredible smile. Onward she went. She was unstoppable. (Kids, don't try this at home!)

After the Great Wall, Beth began to research races around the globe, and contacted foreign organizers to see if they would accept disabled racers with handcycles. Many would, and others would not. She sent out email blasts to her comrades to tell them the results of her findings. Through her perseverance, countries began to accept the disabled racers.

Thus, began her entrance into the 7 Marathons on 7 Continents competition. She was the first disabled woman to race on all continents.

"You and I have been created for greater things. We have not been created to just pass through this life without aim." -
Mother Theresa

Chapter Seven:

Conquering 7 Marathons on 7 Continents

Kilimanjaro Marathon

"It's not the mountain that we conquer, but ourselves." - Edmund Hillary

Kilimanjaro was a grueling race, one high on Beth's list of difficulty. It was held February 24th, 2012, funded by the Challenged Athletes Foundation's Race for a Reason and her own funds from her work part-time coaching athletes and managing the personal training program at a local golf course.

"I traveled by myself to Tanzania and Mount Kilimanjaro and stayed on the coffee bean farm of an ultra-marathon runner. I got food poisoning the night before the race. There I was, all by myself in Africa, sick as a dog, and I didn't have any antibiotics. There was nothing I could do."

She had peanut butter pretzels and started snacking on those. Fortunately, they stayed down. "At 6 AM they came to take me down the mountain for the marathon, and I asked if they had any Coca Cola. They did. I drank a full bottle. I kept the peanut butter pretzels in my back pocket." She made it to the starting line.

The race entailed a serious climb of over two thousand feet. It was sweltering. "If I saw a Coca Cola or Pepsi at one of the stops, I would grab one and keep going. It was a dogfight all the way. I was depleted, and those were the only things I could think of, salt and Coca Cola. I survived and made it." With mind over matter, Beth finished in 4 hours and 53 minutes.

"Everyone wants to live on top of a mountain, but happiness and growth occur while you are climbing it." - Andy Rooney

The disabled racers in the Kilimanjaro race were in need of new racing wheelchairs and handcycles. They were allowed only to race a half marathon. Most of them laid on the side of the road and begged for their needs, and shared food in a church, as well as a shelter, and yet, they wanted to race. So they did.

They were destitute, with few there who were helping with their needs. One of those few was a gentleman named Alex Kiele. Kiele would stay in touch with Beth, who would ultimately give back to his community and the challenged athletes themselves.

You know, many of our traumas come through personal loss, death, divorce, health issues, job losses or financial setbacks. We might not be laying on the side of the road, but we could be laying in bed, eyes wide open, wondering how to cope when something happens. No life is ever free of emotionally and physically painful experiences. There is no way to avoid them. They are part of the reality of existence.

Being traumatized threatens our total equilibrium, especially when the loss is irreversible. What was once accepted as usual and predictable and "present" can vanish.

It takes time to accept the irreversibility of a loss. Great courage is often needed to adapt and carry on. But it can also reveal strengths and resources we never knew we had.

When we take the responsibility for overcoming our traumas, we become better acquainted with ourselves and achieve a greater acceptance of life. A time of pain or loss of hope can be an awakening which opens us up to ourselves, and believe it or not, gives us acceptance of who we truly are. Like the disabled athletes of the Kilimanjaro Marathon, acceptance allows us to move on to create new dreams.

"In time, our pain subsides, our wounds heal, and we discover an all important truth: what remains after all is the most valuable thing we possess, life itself." - Leo Buscaglia

Australian Ross Marathon, Tasmanian

The Australian Ross Marathon, Tasmanian was held September 2nd, 2013. Her time was three hours, 32 minutes. The organizers of the race were amazed that someone in a chair could do it, let alone in the time she achieved. Her performance there opened up the doors for other disabled racers.

> *"My favorite thing is to go where I've never been."* - Diane Arbus

She raised the money for the race through her coaching and fitness management work, and a grant from the Challenged Athletes Foundation.

The Australian Ross Marathon, Tasmanian now allows challenged athletes on handcycles to participate in their marathons.

> *"The marvelous richness of human experience would lose something of rewarding joy if there were no limitations to overcome. The hilltop hour would not be half so wonderful if there were no dark valleys to traverse."* - Helen Keller

Lima, Peru Marathon

The race in Lima, Peru was on May 18, 2013, with funding by the Challenged Athletes Foundation's Race for a Reason, as well as Beth and Burt. Beth was the only disabled participant allowed to do a full marathon in Lima. The other challenged athletes were only allowed to do half marathons. Her time was 2 hours and 18 minutes.

Once again, the poverty of the disabled participants in Lima was shocking. "It was everywhere," says Beth. "They showed up with wheelchair tires covered by glued-on rubber. Duct tape held everything together, even their bodies positioned into the seats of their chairs." Beth was moved by their determination to be a part of the race.

The Peruvians she met had nothing, and lived a day-to-day life, many sharing their wheelchairs and shelter with each other. "I met a wonderful angel of a man named Miguel, of Achilles Peru, who helps provide shelter and meals for them," she says. "Even though the economy has been enriched by tourism and surfing, the Peruvian government does not assist the poor."

But, with Beth's help, the rules for challenged racers were changed. "These athletes are now doing the full marathon with the race director's blessing!"

Over the next year, with Miguel's help and help of friends, Beth found a way to give back.

"If you wait for the perfect moment when all is safe and assured, it may never arrive. Mountains will not be climbed, races won, or lasting happiness achieved." - Maurice Chevalier

Rome Marathon

"Never let the fear of striking out get in your way." - Babe Ruth

The race in Rome was on March 23rd, 2014. It started at the Coliseum. Beth completed it in two hours and 40 minutes. It was a spur of the moment race for her, and she funded it on her own. When she contacted them, she was unsure as to whether they would allow her to race, and at the last minute they accepted her. She decided, "I'll do it."

There were three other disabled women in the race and Beth placed first. The race was in cold rain, and Beth knew not a soul there, but that didn't stop her from making many friends.

Roman "gladiators" greeted her with big smiles at the finish line and informed her that she had won, a complete surprise.

Beth was totally confused when the men acting as gladiators would not give her a race medal as they escorted her to the podium as the first-place female handcyclist. Her confusion turned to her trademark smile as she left with a 2.5 foot trophy.

Later, one of her new-found friends presented her with a race medal for her "7 Continents" collection.

Beth's Return to Rome

Beth was thrilled to be invited to Rome for a second marathon on March 10th, 2016. She finished at two hours and 35 minutes, in second place. Interestingly enough, several months later, she received a package with a first-place medal with no explanation, out of the blue. She couldn't help but wonder if the woman they had given the title to was disqualified. She might never know.

Enrico Castrucci, the race director, had invited her back for this encore race. It was the 20th anniversary celebration of the marathon, and they had asked her and one other woman handcyclist to come join them, as well as handicapped individuals from around the globe. Thirty or more challenged athletes had entered the race, one of whom was a competitor who participated in his racing wheelchair.

Among the challenged athletes who had entered the race was Alex Zanardi, 49, a top Formula One racer, who had been in a severe crash and lost both legs. He was a champion marathoner in Rome in the 90s, and a Paralympian handcyclist who competed in the Rio 2016 games. Zanardi is a humanitarian who started a foundation in Italy that helps challenged children.

Beth loved the Rome Marathon with its amazing beauty and history all along the race route. Rome welcomes handcyclists and race wheelchairs in their marathons, unlike most countries throughout the world.

Racing is life. Anything that happens before or after is just waiting."
– Michael Delaney, character in "Le Mans"

The Boston Marathon

"To be able to look back upon one's life in satisfaction is to live twice." – Kahlil Gibran

Beth's fourth Boston Marathon was held April 20th, 2015. She placed first. "Each time, I have had the honor of riding with the warriors who are wounded from the Achilles

Freedom Team that comes from Bethesda, Walter Reed, and other military rehabilitation hospitals. I am thrilled at this privilege," Beth says.

Nothing you do is ever insignificant." - Aldous Huxley

"The Boston Marathon is my favorite race. For me, it represents the American spirit. It is the homecoming of all races. I truly will keep on doing it until I can't," she says. Her race was funded by the Challenged Athletes Foundation's Race for a Reason and herself.

"There are three simple rules in life:
1.) If you do not go after what you want, you'll never have it.
2.) If you do not ask, the answer will always be 'no.'
3.) If you do not step forward, you will always be in the same place." – Anonymous

Antarctica Marathon

"Life is either a daring adventure or nothing at all." - Helen Keller

The Antarctic Marathon is also called the White Continent Antarctic Marathon. It was February 19th, 2015. Her race was funded by her husband, and Race for a Reason. The jumping off point was Punta Arenas, Chile. She and the other contenders were stranded in the airport there for eleven hours. It took three tries to finally leave because of inclement weather.

When they finally flew to Antarctica, weather delayed their flight and they flew around it for over five hours, and then had to return. Six racers walked out, contenders who were the best of the best. They were competing in a Triple Seven, with 7 Marathons on 7 Continents in 7 Days, and the inability to race in Antarctica on time meant they missed their goal there, and a spot in the Guinness World Records. They were incensed over missing the deadline. The group included CEOs from around the world, executives from the IMF, and Dubai bankers.

Beth finally made it to the continent with 32 able-bodied participants, and spent the night in a tent on rocky ground that she described as a "moonscape." It would be the hardest of the 7 Marathons for her.

"We had boulders that we had to go over, that were iced over, as big as basketballs. I tipped over twice."

As people went by, they asked if they could help her. "No, no don't touch me. Don't touch me because I want to break this record."

She was the only disabled racer. She finished the race in ten hours and 57 minutes, with able-bodied participants cheering her on.

Vietnam Phu Quoc International Marathon

"One's destination is never a place, but rather a new way of looking at things." - Henry Miller

Always an "icebreaker," Beth became a global catalyst in opening up races for other challenged individuals. With every race around the world she was supported and cheered on by so many who believe in her. The Vietnam Phu Quoc International Marathon was held June 11, 2016, and was such a pleasure for Beth. It was her 7th Continent in the official race. She was welcomed graciously by the race director, Marcel Lennartz, who was happy to have a challenged athlete competitor. Originally from The Netherlands, he had been in

Vietnam for 20 years. A former half-Ironman and triathlon competitor, he had started a running club in Ho Chi Minh City. They now hold an Ironman competition, after convincing the South Vietnamese public that races would be a great way to bring in revenues. The marathon took place on the Phu Quoc island, the largest in Vietnam, located in the Gulf of Thailand. It included competitors from 28 different nations. Beth was the only challenged athlete.

Airplane seats are excruciating to Beth, and Phu Quoc was a long journey. She often takes to lying on the floor of an airplane, a position much more comfortable for her spine. All airlines have treated Beth very well, including carrying her handcycles without charge, and being aware of her needs.

It was challenging travel, with 14 hours flying time to Guangzhou, China, and a delay in the air there, circling the airport for 90 minutes as a storm brewed. On the ground, Burt and Beth waited an additional five hours before flying three hours 30 minutes to Ho Chi Minh City. It didn't stop there! Next up was a 45 minute plane ride to Phu Quoc Island. I have no idea how these two do this kind of thing!

The enchanting island of Phu Quoc is a mountainous, lush location for the race. It boasts some of the finest beaches in Vietnam. Beth's race equipment had arrived the day before from China, but was in a not-uncommon situation of taking hours to find. Invariably, in several trips globally, the airlines, gracious in not charging to transport her handcycle, managed to "misplace" it in odd parts of the world en route. In this case, the handcycle had made it, but was lost somewhere. By race day, though, she was good to go.

The race started at the Long Beach Resort Phu Quoc. It was held early in the morning to give competitors cooler racing time. It featured a short off-road segment, in addition to the paved road that made up most of the race. The early start time also gave racers protection from the sun. The race directors describe curvy stretches of the course as "relaxing for the mind" with an "exciting view of the mountains."

"Go" time was at 4:45 AM. The race started and ended at the resort with its beautiful stone driveway. The marathon organizers filmed the start, finish, and the course throughout the race. Cycling in at a time of three hours and 15 minutes, in her signature racing style, Beth blew kisses as she came into the finish line. She was greeted by the general manager of the resort with her first-place award.

A Vietnamese newspaper, television reporters, and film crews surrounded the finish line area to talk with participants and to photograph winners with their trophies. The newscast reached many others in Ho Chi Minh City who have disabilities and could be inspired by it. It was shown all over South Vietnam.

Marcel Lennartz wanted others to know that they can do activities, they can do races, they can live life fully, even with disabilities. The hope is that Beth's participation in the competition will bring out more physically challenged people to come and race. As we know, it is her purpose globally, too.

117

Beth's competitions have taken her all over the world.

"My accident taught me that the term 'success' now means something totally different. I define it in how many lives I can touch and encourage and help."

– Beth Sanden

Chapter Eight:
The North Pole Marathon

"Life shrinks or expands in proportion to one's courage." - Anais Nin

With successfully completing this race on April 9th, 2017, Beth landed in the **Official World Records** as

"First Handcycle Marathons on 7 Continents and the North Pole (Female)."

Beth describes the North Pole Marathon as "an experience of a lifetime," when I interviewed her in a show on YouTube after her return.

"It's almost like you're on a planet that time forgot. It's so calm and quiet and peaceful." I can only imagine the beauty, adrenaline and awe of her time there. Her enthusiasm and energy in describing everything she did and saw, and getting to know the 49 other global competitors, are amazing.

I don't think I've ever heard this level of excitement in her voice and expressions.

"We all met at Longyearbyen, Norway, an island discovered in 1928 by an American miner named Charles Longyear. We stayed in Svalbard, a tiny town on the Island where we were picked up by the Russian paratroopers in a special wooden prop-plane." The plane picked them up in two different groups. These "seasoned" Russian Arctic paratroopers would assist everyone in the compound and along the race course. They would take high ground with rifles to scare off any polar bears in the area if needed.

The snowy white mountains beneath the airplane glistened intensely below the wings. They flew to Barneo Ice Camp, the paratrooper camp near the North Pole. The Russians had gone to the North Pole to prepare it for the marathon. They marked the 90-degree pole and monitored it with a GPS to make sure that they were able to take the contestants to the exact location as the polar ice cap drifted on changes under the earth's crust.

It was clear that Beth had experienced pure joy at the top of the world. Among the 50 competitors were men contenders from the USA, Singapore, Hong Kong, China, Japan, Ireland, Australia, Poland, Italy, Great Britain, Portugal, Russia, Argentina, Nepal, France, and Norway.

The twelve women contenders were from France, Romania, Hong Kong, Finland, Mexico, Italy, Ireland, Great Britain, and the USA.

"For me, this marathon is the grand finale for nine races starting with the Great Wall of China Marathon, my first global one, through the 7 Marathons on 7 Continents, ending with Vietnam in 2016," says Beth. When she was submitting information to Guinness World Records for the 7 Continents, they informed her that she would need to race the North Pole Marathon, as it was a new category they had from the previous two years as "7 Marathons on 7 Continents and the North Pole Marathon." They would give her both titles if she competed successfully. She talked it over with Burt, and he agreed she should jump on it. This changed as she worked with Guinness regarding an award over several months, and ultimately, resulted in the award shown at the beginning of the book.

And so, she embarked on fundraising and training. She was on a mission to prove that a 62 year old disabled woman could show the world that age and disability do not necessarily mean "benched" in life. Beth's goal of showing everyone in the world that they can pursue their dreams is always her mission in everything she does.

The North Pole is defined as a magnetic pole that daily changes position based upon the changes happening under the earth's crust. It's where the earth's axis of rotation meets its surface. There is also the "Terrestrial" North Pole, a fixed point that refers to the very top of our earth. The Arctic is a thin floating ice sheet that constantly changes. In summertime, it decreases its mass by 50%, and in the winter, grows back to its usual size. It sits only one foot above sea level.

Although there is no doubt that the North Pole weather is harsh with its normal high of 32 degrees Fahrenheit, it's in second place for brutality behind Antarctica.

Described in the Antarctic Marathon in previous pages, the window of weather for the marathon there gave them above-zero temperatures, requiring hats and gloves and warm outerwear. Yes, the temperatures were less brutal than the Arctic at the time. However, it took numerous times for the racers to be able to land in Antarctica, due to socked-in unexpected storms over the continent.

The South Pole sits on ice over a piece of land which is Antarctica. Interestingly, the continent of Antarctica is the tallest continent on earth. Who knew? Well, probably a number of you. It's also 9000 feet above sea level. Say what? Unlike the Arctic, temperatures average -76 degrees Fahrenheit in the winter months so, Beth's race there was scheduled for a Southern Hemisphere summertime arrival. At that time, the race route was primarily on plenty of dirt, rock, and some snow and ice.

Like the Scandinavian countries, the North Pole has six months of daylight and six of darkness, something Beth talks about as she describes her trip there. "The sun was so bright, and it was that way 24 hours a day." The sky was an intense blue, and the sun reflected off of the ubiquitous snow.

She trained for the Arctic race in the mountains of California in the snow during early and mid-winter, using steep climbs, and riding through the ice with specially-made handcycle tires designed for traction in snow and ice. "My mantra while I was training was I love wind, I love altitude, and I love cold snow," she says.

The marathon was founded by an Irishman on April 5th, 2002. He raced alone, and then broadcasted it for competitors in 2003. Ten racers signed up. It's considered an ultimate test of a marathoner's ability to overcome the elements. It's nothing new for the 26.2 mile course to experience temperatures seriously below zero, like the -41 degrees Fahrenheit that awaited Beth and the other competitors.

It's a race that attracts few people each year from throughout the globe who want to test their physical limits. The women became instant comrades. The atmosphere in the women's tent was lighthearted and excited. Beth was the only American in the tent, and they called themselves "The Mighty Women of the North Pole." "I was so impressed at how friendly and accepting all of us were. It surprised me." The ladies pulled up social media, swapped stories, took pictures, and laughed heartily as they bonded, each realizing that they were about to experience this amazing feat together. It was a celebration of their kindred spirits and the lifetime connection and memories the marathon would give them.

I told Beth that I'd have a hard time racing any race because I'd need time to put on makeup. She laughed. "Who needed makeup? You weren't able to see faces anyway with the masks and caps."

The racers were taken into the warming tent and then given a tour, and introduced to the small compound of tents with the outdoor latrines, ladies' and men's tents, and a warm rest tent with food.

The ladies' bunks were buried in the racing clothes and gear so high Beth could barely find them. The pile of specialized clothing and gear expanded wall-to-wall without the least bit of complaining from the women. This is their life, symbolic of living it to the fullest. I can only imagine what it was like running from a warm tent to the latrines in -41 degrees Fahrenheit.

When they met for dinner, gathered in the warm food and rest tent at 6:00 PM, the race director welcomed all of them and announced a 10:00 PM start time, as the weather was the best it could be, with little wind. It was April 9th, 2017. They would race into the wee hours of Sunday morning. There was a half-marathon in addition to the full marathon. Several contestants had only triathlon experience, and one racer had never competed in a marathon before. There were a few who had completed half Ironmans, and some who had completed full Ironmans, including Beth. "We didn't sleep before the race. We were running on adrenaline, and we ended up being awake for 48 hours," says Beth.

In this incredible circumstance, all world politics melt away, and the camaraderie that kicks in just to survive in that environment, and to help each other with managing in the hardship, brings the global group together. The ecstatic racers bonded in their tents and in their desire to soak up the whole experience of being there, much of it in the outdoors to be present in the beauty and amazement around them.

"If your actions inspire others to dream more, learn more, do more, and become more, you are a leader." - John Quincy Adams

As Beth finished dressing for the race (I'm sure this was a half hour process), a woman in her 40s from Ireland came to her, and told her that she was so inspired after hearing Beth's story about the accident, paralysis and ultimate racing on her handcycle. She had come to do a half marathon, but changed her mind. "If you can do a marathon with your arms," this woman proclaimed, "I can do the full marathon." She had been diagnosed with a congenital heart problem just four weeks before the race. The doctors were aware of her condition, and she had consulted with the Irish doctor who was there, and Beth asked the American doctor to keep his eye on her, "So she didn't do a face plant!" As they raced and passed each other on the course going opposite ways, she and Beth high-fived each other. She made it across the finish line.

127

The race itself was grueling. Seven hours into it, Beth discovered that her heated gloves had no more working batteries. She had three laps left. She knew that she risked frost bite if she continued, but decided she had come too far to give up the race. She'd take her chances.

Beth crossed the finish line at seven hours and 31 minutes, well before a number of the able-bodied contestants, and yes, with frostbite on two fingers. First place went to Polish runner Piotr Suchenia, at four hours and six minutes. Every racer finished as the temperature dropped to -50 degrees Fahrenheit. 50-below or not, there was a collective rush of happiness, joy, wonder, and sense of accomplishment by 50 people who went immediately to a warm tent with doctors, fellow competitors, and hot food. Beth's two frostbitten fingers were examined and she was given care instructions. Everyone helped finishers warm up, even rubbing feet in the tent. "We were all in this cold together."

Back in the women's tent, the Irish racer with the heart condition waved a flask of celebratory vodka. "She was Irish, after all!" Beth laughed, and passed on it. She had done it. She had finished the race. The elation the contestants experienced bonded them even further and gave them relaxed moments to get to know each other, even with language barriers. You don't have to speak the same language to share the exhilaration of an incredible feat.

And then there was the visit to the North Pole itself. They took helicopters to the exact spot, where they were, literally, on top of the world, doing something that relatively few in history will ever do. The ice cap had drifted, and the North Pole had moved during the race. A satellite shot showed the race pattern shift like an Etch-a-Sketch while the contenders ran the course.

"We were all photographed in our down clothes, face protectors and caps, rendering pretty much all of us incognito," Beth laughed.

"On the way back, we were warm and had been given hot totties and sausage. In the tents, we were snoring from exhaustion. The tents were 'warmed' to about 50 degrees Fahrenheit." Seriously? WARMED to 50 degrees? "I'll never forget the cold," Beth says, "and I never want to feel that cold again."

"We girls were all on the first plane out back to Longyearbyen. From the plane as we left, we could see that the boys would be boys." The men apparently began their own polar bear club. Russian paratroopers chopped through the ice to create a hole and dared each other to jump into the water in their boxers. There was a warming tent nearby like a sauna. A paratrooper was the first into the water. Several of the men went for it.

The humorous follies were watched by the ladies on social media once they had arrived back on Longyearbyen. The women were in hysterics at all of the antics the guys were up to.

During the polar bear fun, a Chinese racer on his belly at the side of the ice hole attempted to take closeup videos of a buddy jumping in. He dropped his phone accidentally into the freezing pool. He was not going to lose his memories of this experience, and immediately slid into the water to retrieve it. The Russians, Americans, and racers from around the world came to his aid, and rushed him into the sauna tent. "We howled," said Beth, "We all laughed and laughed."

Now, *that* is what a bonding at the North Pole Marathon is all about. Across all languages, cultures, ages, and stages of life, we are, in so many ways, the same.

"To walk through life in a comfortable way is not my goal." - Ueli Steck

131

Chapter Nine:
Beth's Commitment to Giving Back to the World

She overcame her enormous difficulties to help others, and you can, too.

"No one is useless in this world who lightens the burdens of others." - Charles Dickens

The Beginning

After months of hospitals, a body cast, going home to her children in a wheelchair, another surgery by a specialist in Colorado, and months more of limited movement, Beth's husband Burt and her Ironman friends threw her into a swimming pool, "You don't have legs, but you have arms," they said, knowing the competitor was still inside her. She swam three to four times a week.

Before long, her friends at the pool announced, "Beth, we're going to do a triathlon relay for this charity called CAF in San Diego. You're going to do this with us. You can do the swim." She was in.

Arriving at stunning La Jolla Cove at sunrise on a beautiful Southern California day for the event, Beth discovered what CAF, the Challenged Athletes Foundation, was about. She was surrounded by the energy of disabled racers from all walks of life. They were there to raise funds for others.

The pre-race music pulsated, demonstration fitness classes were underway, and giveaway booths were in abundance. It reminded her of the excitement and possibilities she had as an able-bodied competitor.

Challenged athletes were everywhere, warriors wounded in deployments, surviving disabled men and women who had lost limbs in accidents, and others with birth defects. CAF had taken over the entire cove. It was full of the life Beth had inside of her, waiting to unleash once again.

The race was a half Ironman, and Beth was to compete in the open ocean water swim for 1.2 miles, where the baton would be passed to a bicyclist, who would then subsequently hand off to a runner for the duration of the race.

Two volunteers carried her onto the beach and into the water, where her legs were submerged. She noticed another woman nearby on the beach who crawled into the water, as most competitors do. She had only one arm, elbow length, and legs that stopped above the knees.

The race began, and the competitor within Beth raced with every ounce of concentration, every fiber of her working limbs, and the rebuilt strength of her heart. She finished the open ocean water swim in 28 minutes, and her competitor with only one arm was carried to the bicycles to transition to the next phase of the race. With the help of her husband, she strapped on two biking prosthetics for the next segment of the race, and off she went.

Beth realized then that this woman, who was more "disabled" physically than she, was a determined challenged athlete who would finish the entire race.

It became a defining moment for Beth.

"Dreams are never destroyed – only rearranged." – Paul Abram Constantine

Beth knew that CAF would give her the avenue and excitement for physical movement that would reignite her passion for racing, as well as the opportunity to help others through its fundraising events.

Her involvement in CAF gave her a new vigor in her daily swims and her regular physical therapy sessions on a treadmill with electrical stimulation to her legs. Then 18 months later, the champion within Beth roared. She regained the use of one leg.

She broke through the excruciating pain and debilitation of paraplegia to become an "incomplete paraplegic," something very few, if any, paraplegics in the world have been able to do. Her wheelchair was benched, replaced by a cane and brace on her left leg for mobility, and the addition of a handcycle for racing. She had overcome the odds with determination, perseverance, courage, and an unbreakable will.

Her presence at fundraising races for CAF, and many other competitions, brings on excitement, energy, and happiness as racers from all walks of life gather alongside her to run or ride in their chairs, on handcycles, or on their prosthetic limbs.

They are drawn to her personal warmth, graciousness, and genuineness. She flashes the magnetic smile that has been her trademark throughout her entire life, greeting participants she knows and introducing herself to those whom she is meeting for the first time.

There's an adage that describes Beth's mission in her outreach: "Be so happy that when others look at you, they become happy, too." Beth has been there, and conquered the pain to return one leg to freedom. That one thing gives these racers enormous hope. She has experienced the incredible feeling of a life outside of her control, and still functions with the monstrously painful result of shattered vertebrae in her past. She knows the sheer willpower it takes to begin to move somehow again. In the disabled athletes world, she is officially a "cheater," their way of teasing her about her success.

"Paying it Back, and Paying it Forward"

Soon, her relationship with the Challenged Athletes Foundation gained new dimensions. Her participation in CAF's fundraising efforts had given her a boost back into life itself.

Now, it gives her ways to express hope and inspiration to others. It has given her a way to give back to others who so desperately want to run and swim and participate fully in life, regardless of their physical and mental disabilities.

"This is what I'm meant to do with my life. I'm paying it back, and I'm paying it forward. My disability has led me to my purpose, and it knows no bounds. There are so many to help and uplift," she says.

Beth "races for a reason" to raise funds for prosthetic legs and arms, racing wheelchairs, and handcycles, all tools to help her fellow disabled friends and acquaintances to achieve their wishes to break free from their constraints.

Beth grew as a global role model for disabled individuals as her racing allowed her to participate around the world, and act as a leader for challenged athletes. Her competitive spirit breaks through global boundaries that disabled individuals experience daily.

For example, as Beth took on bigger and bigger racing goals, she finally made her dream come true: she qualified to race in the 2010 Boston Marathon in the handcycle category, one of four types of disabilities. Her elation was beyond expression, and her fans among the disabled soared in support of her. She did it!

"I want to create opportunities for others, to show everyone that age and challenges can be overcome. It's never too late to achieve your goals and dreams."

We know that in her first Boston Marathon, as one of eight handcyclists who qualified for the race, Beth joined the Achilles Freedom Team affiliated with Bethesda, Walter Reed and other military rehabilitation hospitals. "I was thrilled with the privilege," she says.

She could not resist blowing kisses to the crowd as she cycled through a course lined with spectators. She greeted the fans, who went wild over her presence and watched her race with amazing arm strength on the bike, legs propped up before her, secured to it.

As a role model, she did it. "Challenged athletes are now doing the full marathon with the race director's blessing every year!" she says.

When Beth was invited to the Great Wall of China Marathon, her life was about to change forever. She dove into the unknown, trusting her capabilities, resolve, and the desire to set the world on fire for the disabled, the warriors that have been wounded, accident victims, and all others of us who have been "detoured" in life by circumstances that make it hard for us to achieve our goals and dreams.

Beth did it. So can we.

That amazing marathon had her hooked. She researched and found other competitions around the globe, and communicated with race directors worldwide to see if they would open up the races to her, and then ultimately to challenged individuals.

Upon returning from the Great Wall, Paul and Denise, friends of Beth's who had summited seven of the highest peaks in the world, set the wheels in motion about the "7 Marathons on 7 Continents" competition. During a dinner discussion, they encouraged Beth to think about competing in them.

She found the race organizers, and contacted them to see if they would accept disabled racers with handcycles. Some would not, but Beth can be very persuasive. She was unwilling to take "no" for an answer.

She lit up the inboxes of her comrades with email blasts. She entered the races undaunted by the naysayers, determined to show them throughout the world that she could pass the muster.

She proved herself every mile of the way. She became the first disabled woman in the world to compete in, and complete, all seven marathons. In the process, she did indeed open races worldwide as a role model for challenged participants.

These participants are not just disabled individuals, but disadvantaged as well. As she traveled around the globe with her 7 Continents Marathons, Beth saw the extreme poverty that besets the world, and yet, within this destitution the disabled appeared at the races with broken wheelchairs cobbled together with duct tape and glue. Many had not eaten and had no homes. The possibility of racing was so overpowering even with hungry bellies and physical challenges, they appeared at the starting line. They were elated to be there.

Expanding Her Purpose to Give Back Globally

The Kilimanjaro Marathon

"My worldwide racing taught me that the need for nonprofit talent and assistance is everywhere," says Beth. "It has become my mission to serve."

Each race was an eye-opener for her. As she prepared to compete in the Kilimanjaro Marathon in Tanzania, Africa, Beth was contacted by Kaye Yaffe who wanted to donate water bottles to the other racers. In Tanzania, she met Alex Kilele, Founder of the Kilele Foundation, essentially the equivalent of a 501(c). The Foundation helps the disabled, job seekers, and provides a home for mothers and children. Projects are created to farm, cultivate food and provide clean water. As a child, he had polio, and now walks with braces, but his resolve to be of service to others spilled over into the Kilimanjaro race.

Beth received an email from him before her journey to East Africa, and they arranged a meeting for her arrival and acceptance of the bottles. He traveled from Kenya to

Tanzania to pick them up. "Welcome to Beth Sanden from America, of CAF," said a huge banner upon her arrival at the airport.

On race day, Beth was shocked to see disabled racers arrive in hospital wheelchairs, weighing 40 pounds each, compared to racing wheelchairs designed to weigh in at 14 to 16 pounds. "Alex," she asked, "will these people be racing this 10-mile race, (the distance disabled individuals were told to race) in hospital wheelchairs?" It was her first look at the enormous desire of the disadvantaged and disabled competitors who would surround her in this and other races around the world.

Although the race was grueling for Beth with her food poisoning and its tough elevation changes, she couldn't help but be honored by the enthusisam of Alex and fans, while Alex followed her propped upon a scooter to take photos. Another gentleman held up the "Welcome Beth" sign and followed behind her.

Alongside her, fellow disabled racers in the competition had come out to participate in something that had been previously closed to them. They all raced joyfully and fervently, encouraged by Beth's presence.

Back in the U.S., Beth kept in contact with Alex, and asked if she could help him find equipment for the racers he supports. She reached out to her email network, along with fellow global racers Denise and Paul Fejtek, who reached out to theirs as well. "What if they had older racing chairs and handcycles to donate to Alex for his competitors? Denise, Paul, and I wanted to pay it forward to Alex."

Racing chairs came in from Wyoming, Washington, and Northern California. Then more equipment came in before she left for Africa. She and her racing pals collected extra tires, cables, and everything needed to maintain the equipment. A missionary friend of Beth's suggested they call airlines to ask if their travel could be called a "mission trip."

She connected with airline officials and asked them if she had durable medical equipment to deliver, could the equipment be flown for no charge? Miraculously, Delta, Ethiopian, and LAN airlines told her there was no cost to ship the wheelchairs and handcycles.

Within six to eight months, Denise, Paul, and Beth, along with 20 others planning to climb Kilimanjaro, were able to bring 17 pieces of equipment back to Tanzania to distribute. With Beth's perseverance and performance in the marathon under her belt, she contacted John Addison, race director for both the Kilimanjaro and the Victoria Falls races. She convinced him the disabled were indeed capable of competing in the full marathon. Her performance had changed the race for good.

The following year, disabled competitors in the Kilimanjaro Marathon ALL raced the whole marathon with prize money and medals awarded. Following Kilimanjaro, through her perseverance to compete, the Australia/Tasmania Ross Marathon door opened. Beth traveled "down under." The organizers were amazed she could do it, let alone in the time she achieved. Once again, we know her performance there paved the trail for other disabled racers. They now allow challenged athletes on handcycles to participate in their marathons.

With Burt's urging, Beth had decided she would donate her own handcycle, along with a regular wheelchair and a racing chair to Tanzania after she completed the Australian marathon. As the "diplomat" for the trip, as Burt explained it, she made one more journey to see Alex and the racers. She delivered the equipment to him amongst fanfare and a banquet he had arranged. Beth's sense of purpose soared to new heights.

The Lima, Peru Marathon

"Life's most precious and urgent question is 'What are you doing for others?'" – Martin Luther King

Burt accompanied Beth to the Lima marathon on May 18, 2013, and they were the first to arrive at the starting line. They had not seen any racers beforehand, but at the starting line, out of the blue, a group of disabled racers approached and surrounded her. She had met "Miguel Achilles Peru," the President at the Achilles International Peru, another group like CAF, prior to the race. Achilles International aids physically disabled racers. He introduced Beth and Burt to them, as they gathered around her.

They were mesmerized by Beth's handcycle. You might remember from the Lima race description that the poverty of the disabled participants in Peru was shocking. Their racing cycles were dilapidated, and their wheelchairs were held together with glue and duct tape. But to Beth, she saw an amazing group who were doing all they could with what they didn't have. They bounded into the start of the half marathon race and were going for it every mile of the way.

Beth, the only disabled racer allowed to compete in the full marathon, was cheered as she crossed the finish line. She was greeted and joined by an ecstatic crowd who wanted to meet her and take photos with her. Once again, her presence and what it meant to their lives gave them enormous joy.

On her visit, Beth could not believe the level of destitution she saw. Miguel would help provide shelter and meals. She discovered that wheelchair-bound individuals would often share them. The needs of Peru's disabled athletes became another charitable cause for her.

Back home, once again, Beth began to ask her connections for help. She contacted Achilles International in New York City to ask about equipment, and worked with the Challenged Athletes Foundation in California as well.

They did email blasts to find older equipment still in great working order. It took Beth nine months to find four pieces of equipment, which would be transported with Paul and Denise, who were traveling to climb Machu Picchu. Another friend, a missionary traveling to Peru, donated two more pieces and took the equipment with him. Beth, who competed in the Antarctic Marathon, accompanied three pieces of the equipment to deliver to Miguel.

All told, she collected nine pieces of equipment. Miguel, searching for a way to store the equipment as it came in, found a builder who donated an office building to use as an

Achilles Peru headquarters. He could house it there. They were one step closer to helping the disabled who wanted racing as part of their lives to soar with pride and enthusiasm.

Beth's work with the Challenged Athletes Foundation (CAF)

Throughout all of Beth's racing, there has been one central theme: to show the world that warriors who have been wounded, accident victims who have been paralyzed or lost limbs, or both, the brain injured, and individuals with birth defects long to move like the able-bodied and want to be seen with their disabilities. They often go faster with more enthusiasm and sheer contagious willpower than their able-bodied competitors.

"I'm determined to set the example and prove to us all that we can participate in life fully, and resurrect our dreams by racing in the unknown and successfully conquering every goal," she says. She is her challenged counterparts' biggest fan as they, too, surpass their limitations and experience the bliss of a sense of accomplishment that is incomprehensible to us able-bodied.

Let their accomplishments be the inspiration to achieve your dreams. She will be *your* biggest fan, too, as you vow to conquer your own difficulties while striving to fulfill a sense of purpose. Purpose is a powerful thing. Beth shows us just how powerful it can be.

"You know I believe that the nonprofit need for talent is so important," says Beth. "CAF was the perfect charity for me. You could say that I discovered it because I needed to figure out what was next for me."

Her desire to help CAF fundraise, and to encourage others, led Beth to compete in those 78 marathons and 70 triathlons. What an astounding example of commitment, dedication, and purpose! She is our hero and our champion. If *she* can do that feat, we can do our feats, too.

With many of these, she raised funds and awareness for CAF's mission through "Race for a Reason" in marathons such as Kilimanjaro, Lima, Boston, and Antarctica. CAF's "Race for A Reason" allows both able-bodied and disabled racers alike a way to raise money for the population it serves.

The CAF organization is an important body for raising funds to help individuals with physical challenges realize their dreams of having active lifestyles.

Their mission is to provide opportunities and support for the disabled to pursue physical fitness and competitive athletics. "CAF believes that involvement in sports at any level increases self-esteem, encourages independence and enhances quality of life," it states.

There are one billion people worldwide who are disabled, 15% of the earth's population, according to a study by the

World Health Organization with the World Bank. The 2015 U.S. Census Bureau reports that there were 40 million disabled in the US - nearly 13% of our population. CAF gives them a way to participate in life that boosts their self-confidence and self-esteem. CAF helps them conquer their disabilities in a number of ways.

CAF provides grants to fund adaptive equipment, clinics, and mentorship to help individuals achieve their goals to get moving again and to get back into life. CAF needs the support of volunteers to keep it vibrant and accessible in continuing its mission well into the future, helping more and more challenged athletes.

Their fundraising is robust, and 80% of every dollar expended by the Foundation goes to their mission.

CAF's Program Services are extensive to meet the needs of challenged individuals who are ready to race, and to become Challenged Athletes. The programs CAF offers include:

- The **Military Operation Rebound** provides equipment, stages events and gives resources to veterans.

- **Access for Athletes** provides equipment and grants.

- **Catch a Rising Star** sponsors the Dodge Camp Discover, and Dodge Para-triathlon Camps.

- **Dodge Swim Clinics**, Ossur Leg Amputee running clinics, and wheelchair clinics.

- **Reach High** provides educational tours.

- **Jeff Jacobs Challenged Athlete Center** and events.

- **Project Next** is devoted to serving San Diego County in Southern California. Beth was fortunate enough to race in a few of her competitions because of grants from CAF, which helped her meet the challenge of being the first disabled woman to race all seven continents, plus The Great Wall of China Marathon, and the North Pole Marathon.

CAF's grant distribution:

The grants are critical to help challenged individuals get the equipment and prosthetics they need to be active, which are cost-prohibitive to most. How many grants did CAF give to challenged athletes in 2017?

- 2,448 grant recipients were approved in 2017, for a total of $3.7 million in distribution.

- Military support was given $478,929.00 in grant funds.

- Equipment requests were granted for 97 sports.

How were the grant dollars distributed? Here are tallies of a few:

267 Wheelchair basketball grants
190 Track and field grants
112 Beep baseball grants
82 Triathlon grants
79 Wheelchair rugby grants
78 Handcycle grants
78 Cycling grants
73 Swimming grants

What is the breakdown of physical disabilities receiving grants?

20% Amputees
17% Paraplegics
15% Visual Impairment
11% Spina bifida
10% Cerebral palsy
27% Other

Beth gives back to support CAF and its continuous efforts through her volunteer work. It fuels her, and gives her an outlook for her passion to help others. This involvement reminds us that we, too, can contribute to a cause that resonates with us, that stirs our passions, and the desire to have an impact while helping to fulfill the needs of others.

Beth's outreach within her community and throughout the world

Throughout the year, her community outreach is an initiative she pursues with rigorous enthusiasm as well.

"I enjoy speaking to schools, companies, and professional organizations such as Kiwanis, Women's Clubs, the Elks, the Rotary Club, and Garden Clubs.

I speak regularly to colleges, adaptive PE Programs, hospital rehab facilities for the disabled, triathlon clubs, and more. It's all about raising awareness on behalf of those in need, and I love doing it," she says. The speeches focus on raising awareness about CAF.

Her creation of Paratriathlon Camps

At home, Beth works with challenged athletes who want to participate in events. It's how she thrives in giving back.

"I don't have a lot of money, but I have a lot of joy. When I see someone I coach cross the finish line, it gives me a rush of happiness." She says she's living her truth, and her purpose is to be authentic and to give back. "It's what I'm here to do."

Beth is one of only four disabled Certified Triathlon Coaches in America, and she decided to use her credentials to conduct her own Orange County, California (OC) Paratriathlon Camps once a month, January through September, each year.

For four years, she has invited a spectrum of disabled participants, ranging from those with no sports history at all, to seasoned disabled racers, to join in her program.

She charges nothing to coach her participants.

Within the camps, disabled individuals can learn three different disciplines in tiers of difficulty. Some are beginners and children who have never swam, and they need to start with swimming first. Some want to learn cycling; others to use push wheelchairs.

"If I can get those who have never swam with their disability to learn to swim, we go down to the ocean at beautiful La Jolla Cove in San Diego, and let them feel the freedom of swimming toward a goal. If I'm working with more experienced challenged athletes who want to go to the next level and cross finish lines in their racing goals, it's all so rewarding to me."

In January 2017, ten people began the camp. The number varies each time, and she has had as many as twelve in one camp. In some camps, she has had individuals who were training to do the Ironman California within a few months.

As you now know, it's a grueling race to even able-bodied entrants, with its 2.4-mile swim, 112-mile bicycle race, and topped off with a full marathon. Her participants aspire to move on to other races as well.

"When I'm with them, especially in the water, whether with two legs, or one; one arm or two, it doesn't matter what their disability is, I see no limitations. It's wonderful to see it click with them. They might start low, but they end high."

Beth keeps her connections in the loop about starting dates for the camp each year through Facebook posts, email, and Instagram. She also posts the growth of the group members' skills, communicates with them through Facebook, as well as messaging them with individualized lesson plans for the programs she creates for each.

They meet once a month for progress evaluations, and at the close of each four-month period, for those who have come to learn to swim, there are swimming critiques.

Then, with confidence high, they are ready for their ocean debut.

Beth was named "Volunteer Coach of the Year" by USA Triathlon four times for creating her OC Paratriathalon Camps in 2010, 2011, 2013, and 2014.

An Encourager For the Rest of Us

Beth also meets with 24 disabled friends and new acquaintances quarterly at one of their homes to have lunch together and collaborate on how to live with their disabilities. They're disabled from accidents or birth defects.

"When I was first in the wheelchair, I noticed that people just looked over the top of my head and didn't look at me or acknowledge me. They're uncomfortable being around the disabled and can't even say 'hello.' I became invisible, as my friends became invisible. Being in a 'chair' can be a lonely experience."

She knows that the best gift you can give a disabled individual is a smile and a greeting, directed expressly at their eyes.

> *"Personally, looking around, I don't even see a disability. I see a total human being, a whole person."* - Beth

"My new friends, as well as disabled friends I've known for several years now, are in varying states of disability. Some are quadriplegics, and I encourage them to remember that even one tiny movement is an accomplishment to be shared and celebrated." It's another one of the gifts she gives - encouragement. After her own feat of bringing one leg back to life, she knows the power of encouragement, even if it's given only once a month, from her.

Beth's husband had helped her see that she could be a positive blessing to other disabled individuals, because so many were thirsting for her words of encouragement. Not everyone can move on from the trauma of becoming disabled. They can be stuck with the inability to see any future for themselves.

"My body is now a tool to help others. I talk to them. I acknowledge that they're still here participating in their lives. I commend them on their activities and hopes for the future. I'm still here. There is a lot of life in us."

Oftentimes, disabilities are because of depression, bipolar disorder, or any one of other conditions that able-bodied individuals have as well.

"One gentleman I know has been trying to deal with his bipolar disorder. He has been taking medication and starting to go out to the beach. It's changing his whole world. He's living life more fully, one tiny step at a time. I'm so proud of him."

Her disabled friends in wheelchairs also tease her about being a "cheater" because she made it out of the chair by using one leg. "It takes a while for all of us who become disabled to process what this means, and to try to change our circumstances to the best of our ability to get back into life," she says. "I have one friend who was told she would be in a chair for the rest of her life. She is now using her arms in a push-assist chair. She is an incomplete quadriplegic, and to her, this is a joyous achievement."

"I tell her, and all of my challenged friends, that once we have a victory in a small movement, we need to decide: What can I make of it, and what can I do with it? How can I make it count? She can be more active as a mother. It took her about five years to decide she's in a pretty good place. She can participate fully within her world, with whatever she has achieved in movement," says Beth.

Beth knows that it's one step forward, one step backward for the newly handicapped. "My amputee friends must go through a series of surgeries and can often make it back to crutches. Many amputees have been through losing their limbs to cancer. Once they can embrace the fact that they have a new normal, they will realize it's time to move on back into life again."

"It's not money or prestige. It's much simpler than that. Person to person, I help each one of us to take even the tiniest step toward more ability. That's success! The other day I was on handcycles with amputees and paralyzed friends, and we were all over with our bikes and prosthetics. It's the new normal and we embrace it and even have fun with it."

She's living with purpose and living her dreams. "What are you waiting for? We don't know how long we have here. Make every day count. When they told me I'd never walk again, they also told me the accident would shorten my life span. So what?"

"I now live my life moment by moment. All of us can create opportunities for ourselves to succeed at something, whether tiny or huge. And we can decide to write our own endings for our hopes and dreams."

Beth now has a plaque above her doorway: "Attitude is everything. Pick a good one." She has one. Her constant beaming smile is proof .

Her racing is not her only contribution to helping others. Beth's smile, greetings and attention to each of us as she walks with her cane, and swings her still paralyzed left leg to greet us, one by one, lights *us* up with motivation. There is a reason Beth is here: to help, to coach, to inspire, and to open new worlds for us, literally, across the globe.

Chapter Ten:
How Can You Give Back in Your Own Life?

"Happiness is not something you get, but something you do."
- Marcelene Cox

Beth Sanden is a role model for ALL of us. Think about how and why you want to contribute. Think of all that Beth endured before she realized that the role of giving back to those in need among the disabled gave her such happiness and sense of accomplishment that she now spends her life in pursuit of ways to give back.

Numerous studies show that giving back is the antidote to feelings of depression or hopelessness, and can energize those of us who believe we have lost our dreams or our ability to meet our goals, and to all of us who have been "detoured" by life. Perhaps we must drop everything to take care of a parent with Alzheimer's. Perhaps we lost a job and had a grueling search to find something, anything, to help pay the bills. Perhaps we were detoured with cancer treatment and surgeries.

It's proven that volunteering to help others in any cause you choose will lift you out of your worries and give you a new outlook on your value.

You wouldn't be alone, as Americans are givers with both volunteer work and money. The statistics might already include you. Sixty-three million Americans volunteered in 2017, putting in nearly eight billion hours of volunteer time.

I discovered that The National Philanthropic Trust has measured giving rates of Americans for several years, and it is inspiring:

- The average American household gives over $2000 per year to their passionate causes.

- In 2017, Americans gave overall approximately $410 billion to charitable causes.

- 70% of all donations are made from individuals like Beth, me and you; then foundation donations of 16%, bequests at 9%, and corporate donations at 5%.

- We are all, as individuals, impacting the world more than any other entities. Charitable giving by individuals in 2017 was nearly $287 billion.

Beth encourages us to get involved and to consider a cause that's in sync with our experiences, beliefs, or hobbies. So many need our help. Let yourself think about what would be the perfect charitable cause for you.

Maybe it could be Alzheimer's Disease. You might even be a caretaker right now for a loved one with the challenging degenerative disease.

- Every minute, someone in America is diagnosed with Alzheimer's. Over 16 million caregivers put in over 18 billion unpaid hours in caregiving for Alzheimer's and other dementias. 83% of caregivers are family members. 40% of them have college degrees.

- 25% of Alzheimer's caregivers are also caring for children 18 and under. They are called the "sandwich generation" caregivers. They are caring for parents and their children all at once.

- Sadly, 250,000 caregivers are from eight to 18 years old.

- It's often called the "caregiver's disease" because of the emotional exhaustion caretakers experience while providing daily assistance. 74% of them are concerned about maintaining their own health, and indeed, spend approximately $10 billion in their own healthcare per year.

- It's a tough job, and it's often in addition to paid work done five days a week. They're overloaded.

There are groups to join that will give you the chance to assist caretakers with their exhaustion and give them practical services like grocery shopping and errand assistance. Many organizations now have daycare centers for Alzheimer's and dementia patients who are living with their families, giving caretakers "timeouts" from their work. There are retreats for caregivers that give them the opportunity to relax and rejuvenate while attending educational workshops.

All of these need volunteers to help "care for the caregivers."

If you are an experienced family caretaker for an Alzheimer's patient yourself, perhaps you could mentor others who have found themselves caught up in the crisis of a dementia or Alzheimer's diagnosis. Every year, as the cases increase, more members of your community need to know what you already know about caretaking.

No, exhausted caregivers are not the only cause. It just happens to be huge and growing. You know there are many other causes desperately needing support. For example, you've also learned here about helping disabled individuals live a fulfilling life.

Check out these possible charitable causes. Which one will touch your heart enough to reach out to others and volunteer?

- Is it children's care for diseases and disabilities?

- Is it feeding the hungry or clothing the poor?

- Is it bringing blankets to the homeless on freezing nights?

- Is it breast cancer research and assistance to patients?

- Is it mission work?

- Is it heart disease or diabetes?

- Is it helping disadvantaged families build homes?

- Is it wild animal and/or pet causes?

- Is it finding ways to help others with job search assistance?

- Is it helping the organizations who are advocates for the mentally ill, or those with other brain disorders?

- Is it helping veterans?

- Is it environmental causes?

These causes touch an untold amount of hearts, as do many, many others. Perhaps you've chosen even more than one.

Find something you can be passionate about. It will help bring you back to life if you are experiencing a traumatic detour, disappointment or discouragement. Helping others is truly a way of helping yourself. Each of us can mean the world to someone else, no matter what our conditions, circumstances, and challenges.

Therein lies an ability to experience our own healing and happiness, just like Beth.

EPILOGUE

Joy and Purpose

"Life was not meant to be easy, but take courage: it can be delightful." - George Bernard Shaw

Joy:

"A feeling of great pleasure and happiness." - The English / Oxford Dictionaries

This book about Beth Sanden and how she overcame her own disappointments, discouragements, and detours to resurrect her purpose, is not just about the racing. It's about how she found completeness and joy as a paraplegic, with a renewed sense of purpose along with a "new normal."

At the same time, this book is about *you*, with encouragement and tips for resurrecting your own purpose, or for finding new ones as you change throughout life.

It is, just like Beth's life, an inspiration for you to live your purpose and find joy.

Pure and simple, joy is the most wonderful experience on the planet, and sometimes off the planet as well! I'm sure every astronaut knows the meaning of joy!

Joy is part of Beth Sanden's life. Joy is who she is. It's a trademark that drives her smile and genuine connection with everyone she meets. Beth is the essence of authenticity, a quality that draws us to her. She accepts all of us for who we are. We are all changed by knowing her. Authenticity is something we explore in this epilogue as well.

Every race has given Beth joy. Each of Beth's races means something unique and special to her. Every paratriathlon camp she holds and every challenged athlete she trains give her joy as she watches participants swim, bike or run. Sometimes they've never dreamed that they could do it. Their exultant happiness and sense of achievement spill over from her onto them and from them onto her. It's magnetic. And it's all because she is purpose-driven to do something greater than herself.

Living your purpose is a joy-powered experience. Imagine the joy Beth felt in the Arctic, connecting with a brave few who decided to conquer it, all pumped up with adrenaline, and ecstatic to be there. As I mentioned before, when I interviewed her for a YouTube segment about the North Pole Marathon, I realized that the joy in her voice and expression are so powerful, they can open up listeners to joy as well.

Part of her purpose as she races is to connect with as many authentic individuals as she can. These include other purpose-driven contacts from around the globe. Some run charities to help the disabled. Some donate to help via the Challenged Athletes Foundation. Some contribute needed racing equipment and supplies to those disabled individuals around the world who have nothing but the clothes on their backs. They want to become active as challenged athletes in wheelchairs taped together with duct tape, and hopeful smiles on their faces, even though they are not the fastest racers by any means. It's glorious to them. They do it for their own joy.

Each race on the map connects her with more and more new friends who want to help them, more and more who want to do something greater than who they are.

That's the thing about purpose and joy. The energy of their presence is so uplifting they have the power to transform us. Joy has the power to save us. It's life-changing. It's a life force. The cool thing about joy is that it's not powered by laws of scarcity. It has no beliefs that there will never be enough money, or happiness, or food, or peace in your life. It has no judgment that you can never be what you really want to be. It has no impression that you'll never be able to shed your current circumstances, that you are chained to them for the rest of your life. Joy is the antidote. Purpose can put it into action.

When Beth decided to start entering races around the world, she knew she had found her true calling. Each race gave her so much joy using her God-given talents and feeling the strength of her purpose. Was it easy to make such a decision? Only in the sense that once she started the races, and met challenged individuals everywhere who wanted to be racing like she was, she and Burt realized that her racing must continue on. She realized that her racing is who she is, and what she's meant to do. Burt expressed to her that it was clear to him that she is a world ambassador for spreading the message that the disabled can do what they dream of, and be in their own purpose. They can come out of the shadows and run, swim, bike, play sports, and just be who they are in the presence of everyone in their communities and beyond.

Beth and Burt are wealthy in spirit, wealthy in love, wealthy in family, wealthy in faith, and wealthy in friendships. They joyfully send Beth wherever she is called to be in her purpose. They fund Beth's worldwide races with their own hard work. And sometimes they are blessed with donations or grants from CAF and other organizations. They take the leap each time, focusing on the joy in their decision, believing in their faith and intent.

Purpose:

"A person's sense of resolve or determination." and *"Have as one's intention or objective."* - Oxford Dictionaries

I think the biggest lesson we can learn from Beth's joy is that if you dig deep enough into yourself and acknowledge your purpose and embrace it, joy might start poking around you. If it does, reach out to it. Take it and hold on. Joy is not selfish. It loves to multiply and give itself as we extend our hands to it. Although we might experience joy as a quiet "knowing" within us, the truth is that joy is as active as a basketball game. It is not an elusive emotion, playing hide-and-seek. Rather, it's right in front of us, waiting for us, patiently, to say "yes" to it.

We can have parallel challenges in our own lives that can possibly be our own Waterloos. Ultimately, we can overcome them with a resurrected purpose, or by creating a new one. Yet many of us search for it, and feel like we come up empty-handed. How can we change that? Well, let's look to Beth for inspiration. She did it one small step at a time. We don't have to expect that it will come overnight. Beth had her own "Ah ha!" moment when she realized that her purpose was unfolding before her. Perhaps we can do it, too? We can certainly take a look at ways to resurrect a purpose-driven life.

Let's talk about examples of disappointments, discouragements, and detours that can affect our ability to find, recreate, or perhaps accept, purpose and joy in our lives.

We can be blindsided by life's difficult, unexpected events.

Ladies and gentlemen, I usually try to be as erudite as possible when I write, but sometimes life just sucks.

Ah, yes. Has the breakup of a relationship thrown you off your game? Do you feel like everyone else is happy in their marriages, and you're not capable of nurturing a successful one? Do you feel like your breakup makes you a failure?

Or, do you struggle with the bills, often created by your own spending? Sometimes it is necessary for survival. But it's still oppressive. We can feel irresponsible, and "less than," while we chastise ourselves for being in that position. The recent Great Recession put many of us in that situation, in a tailspin, and living paycheck to paycheck.

Have you been fired or laid off at work? Have your self-esteem, purpose and joy taken a terrifying nosedive? This is a big one. So many of us feel our purpose is in our work.

When you lose a job due to layoff or being fired, your self-esteem can go down the drain, and any joy you had from bringing home the bacon to support your family can evaporate. To top it off, the financial hit can be devastating to you and your family. Perhaps you have toddlers to feed, or teenagers cleaning out the fridge. Perhaps you are in a different stage of life, have kids in college, or just out of college, and you are helping to pay back school loans. Everyone around you feels the stress.

You may feel that you don't have a grasp on your purpose anymore, and you might not realize that a new one can emerge, or you can resurrect the one you've had. Your purpose could be right there knocking at the door, and you can open it, say "hello," and invite it in.

We all know that no matter what the job loss circumstances, breakups, or money problems, we're on a journey that feels just plain lousy. We can feel embarrassed. We can feel humiliated. We must reinvent ourselves with resolve and perhaps a renewed sense of purpose. Then we get back in the game. Keep going!

Our lives are turned upside down with devastating news about our own, or a loved one's, health.

Boy, does Beth know this one. She was told by doctors that she would spend the rest of her life in a wheelchair. Like her and her family, we have to evolve within a new normal. Her life is an example that we can break through to a purpose, and that it's achievable. Have the resolve to believe it.

Beth's entire family's life changed dramatically in an instant with her accident, and it wasn't easy for them to move forward into an uncertain future. Joy might have become a fleeting concept. However, in their case, they learned to find the joy again with their faith. You might find it in another way. Beth's capabilities evolved and her purpose lifted the family's life with love and enthusiasm, and plans for the future. It wasn't all roses, but her lifetime of authenticity still shone brightly. Her purpose became more and more focused as well, as she trusted that she was to race and give back globally. With every step she takes, the world changes for the better.

With each day that goes by, Beth is changing lives with her purpose, and helping others to have a purpose themselves. Individuals whose lives have changed from accidents, rendering them amputees. Individuals with birth defects that leave them with partial arms or legs. Warriors who are wounded in battle. Seniors who have always wanted to do marathons. Literally everyone who is determined to get back into life. This is the power of resurrecting your purpose. Do it in the now, wherever you are, whatever your path.

So, how do we bring purpose and joy into our lives right now?

Below are some simple ways you can bring purpose and joy into your life. Not all of them will suit you, but I encourage you to think about them and consider other ways that might work for you personally. You might also be surprised to learn that some, even though you might never have thought about them, could work very well for you if given the chance.

Remind yourself that joy doesn't only come into our lives with the big stuff.

Starting small is fine, because it's still starting. And just starting is the key.

- That's one of the best things about joy. It has no size requirement.

- Beth knows well that you do not need to "earn" joy.

- Everyone can embrace it if they want it. It's yours, it's mine, it's a stranger's, it's everywhere around the world. Beth has experienced it everywhere and it has given her so much.

- Joy is a connector. It's one thing that can be totally in common with all of us on the planet. It's not its size, it's how much it's shared.

Have you heard about the Christmas truce among German and British soldiers in Belgium in World War I, when both sides of the conflict put aside their arms for that special time? It started with the Germans singing Christmas carols and shouting Christmas greetings from their trenches to the English soldiers, who at first were wary of what was happening.

Soon they realized that the Germans truly were reaching out to them with Christmas wishes. Little Christmas trees were appearing along the tops of the German trenches. The soldiers were joyous about having a break from war. In order to celebrate the theme of "peace on earth," even mortal enemies laid down their arms for camaraderie. It's an amazing story about troops who were battle-weary and had lost their desire for conflict. This gave them a respite, and joy.

Yes, we have times in our lives when it seems we are unable to find joy or express it. Hang on. Oftentimes, joy sneaks in a door we didn't know was open. It can be a nice surprise.

Gratitude:

"The quality of being thankful; readiness to show appreciation for, and to return kindness."

Be grateful for something daily, anything, big or small in your life.

Can you imagine the enormous gratefulness Beth experienced when, after months of excruciating pain, swimming, and physical therapy, she was able to leave her wheelchair behind? She mastered the use of one leg, first with a walker and then a cane. This one leg created an ability to walk by swinging her still totally paralyzed leg forward as she ambulated. I can only imagine the joy. It gave Beth the opportunity to pick up the pieces of who she is and move forward into the future with a resurrected purpose to help others, and to be an excellent role model.

I express my gratitude for the life I have every single day. I say it out loud. I express it for my husband's love and hard work to keep me comfortable, happy and with necessities. I'm grateful for the health of my body, which lets me hike and enjoy the outdoors, and to attend tough exercise classes. I have for years been grateful for beautiful skies as I open my blinds each morning. I'm so grateful for my siblings, many wonderful friendships, and a roof over my head. I express gratitude for Miss Kitty, who welcomes me every time I wake up, and stretches to greet me.

This is just the tip of the iceberg for my gratefulness, but it's the first list of thanks I express upon waking. These are the most important things in my life.

Make your own gratitude list.

Try doing this, if you haven't before. Start your day by finding something to be thankful for, even if it's miniscule. Or you can *end* each day with the same.

Your gratitude list will undoubtedly be very different than mine. Perhaps you express gratitude for a baby, your job, for your spouse, your children, and your grandchildren. Maybe you are grateful for your mother and father, and the wonderful life lessons they taught you. Or perhaps your garden of flowers, or vacations. You might express it in the morning like I do, or at night as you retire.

It could be, like me, you express gratitude for your pets and their playfulness, personalities, the way they make you laugh with their antics, and their unconditional love. My sister has a morning routine every day that gives her joy, a gratitude experience, with her Golden Retriever and Bengal kitty.

The Golden scarfs down his bowl full of food, and the Bengal jumps into my sister's lap as she has her coffee. She has a bag of treats for her kitty that she hides in the pockets of her robe and there is a playful routine that unfolds and grabs the Golden's attention at her feet. It's peaceful, fun and makes her start her day with laughter. She is so grateful for it.

If you focus on the things you're grateful for, you can think about them whenever the tough moments come around. You can write them down in a journal if you wish, or place them on your bathroom mirror to keep the list in front of you daily. Add to it when you have the "Ah ha!" moment about another thing you're grateful for.

Now, this is one of the most important things about expressing gratitude: when you are reviewing the things you are grateful for, there is no room for thinking negative thoughts. Try speaking your gratefulness out loud. You'll notice that you can't speak a gratitude list, and negative thoughts, simultaneously. It's either/or. Choose the gratitude list.

There is no contest or concept of big or small when it comes to gratitude. There is no competition with anyone else, because no two of us are alike, nor should we be. We are definitely often in the same circumstances and can be helpful to one another, but we'll still have our own unique gratitude list.

What's yours? Can you make a list, even if you're grateful just for a breather with a cup of coffee each morning? (By the way, that's on my list, too.) This can lift your spirits every day.

If you wonder what's powerful about making a gratitude list, it's this: gratefulness gives you a positive perspective, directly linked to joy and purpose. Gratitude keeps you in the present moment, without casting worry about what the future holds. It's all about being thankful for the here and now, which is the only point in time we can be absolutely sure of.

Grateful positivity creates action, and your purpose grows out of it. What you feel is important to you is the direction you can go for resurrecting or creating it. You're taking time to focus on what you value in life, and if you follow where it takes you, look for your purpose. It will be there.

As Goethe said, *"Whatever you do, or dream you can do, begin it. Boldness has genius, power, and magic in it."*

Get outside. Take a walk.

How wonderful it is that Beth lives most of her life outside in the breeze, in ocean air, in the cold, in the desert, on islands, and at the poles of the earth.

You needn't drive to an "official" place to be outside. Remember the days when we used to "get outside" in our backyards and our neighbors' yards? We used to sit around logs on the fire on lawn chairs with conversation. It was a way of refreshing ourselves and it still can be. At the same time, our lives could be full of walking as well. We kids walked to school, which was great for our energetic burn off. We built treehouses and explored the woods all around us. I remember walking everywhere with a girlfriend. We had legs and we used them.

So, just walk out your front door. Look at your surroundings with new eyes. Are you seeing things you've never noticed? What about trees? Grass? Are there wildflowers along the way? What other kinds of plants do you notice? Take it in. What about squirrels or chipmunks? Is there birdsong? What are the skies like? What are the neighbors' homes like? Do you find any of particular inspiration? Perhaps the paint color, or the design of the doorstep, or the garden?

Say "hi" to passersby. Do you see neighbors that you routinely wave to as you drive by, but have never spoken to them? Now is the time. Make a new friend close by, who shares the surroundings with you. Greet everyone who has a dog. I'm serious, I swear by this one. It's one of the quickest ways to make new friends and both dog and pet parent will love the attention. Which reminds me, be sure to take your own pooch with you when you go. There's nothing like an enthusiastic companion.

Then take this walk, or mix it up and go a different route, as often as you can, maybe once a week? Then twice a week, and then three times a week? You will find many things outside that can give you joy. And the health benefits are the best.

Studies show that a brisk walk several days a week is at least as good, or better, for you than hard exercise. Plus, there's the added benefit of your brain being cleared of stress, and open to new thoughts about tackling any challenges that you have, and new ways of doing things. The bottom line is that you can actually think without distraction. Many an answer to life's stresses comes to us when we are outside of our usual space, taking a walk.

Finally, invite a friend, spouse, sibling, or neighbor to go with you. Process your thoughts and challenges together. Let it all help you melt stress, imagine solutions to problems, and inspire you to dream. That's what taking a walk can do for you. And what can you do to bring yourself a morsel of joy? Perhaps surround yourself with the flowers you've seen and loved?

Oh, and by the way? Keep your phone tucked away if you bring it, and just be present in the walk itself.

Even if you live in the heart of the city, there is still plenty for you to notice with new eyes. I know that when I lived in Manhattan, I saw the city with new fascination every day.

In the Arizona desert, my father loved to take walks around the neighborhood and look for interesting rocks. Amazingly, rocks feature all kinds of designs, patterns and uniqueness. In one rock you'll see a face design. In another, you'll see the Rock of Gibralter. In another, you'll see something else. Rocks are like clouds. When you look at them, you see many different things in their shapes and sizes.

Well, instead of grass for his yard work, my father would take these rocks and create individual rock gardens throughout our front and back yards. It was his art, for everyone to enjoy and be surprised at his depth of design. Something as simple as a rock gave him joy, and making rock gardens gave him a purpose each day. It started with walking and observing his neighborhood and the desert features, like endless amounts of rocks.

When you start a walking habit, you will realize how isolating it is to spend your life in a vehicle. Instead, you can easily connect with many others, and so much beauty and wonder that you had often driven right past.

"The invariable mark of wisdom is to see the miraculous in the common."
Ralph Waldo Emerson

Connect with others daily.

Make it your purpose to be attentive and loving and to do the best job you can *where you are* at the time, and to take care of your own needs for connection to others.

Beth is absolutely a connector. She has been connecting all of her life. She becomes *more* with each race, better, kinder and stronger. Each competition she enters, wherever in the world, brings her the opportunity to increase her share of connections. These often become lifelong comrades, full of inspiration for her as well.

"The best way to cheer yourself up is to try to cheer somebody else up." - Mark Twain

For some of you, you feel deeply about, and love, the sense of purpose that having a job, or being a caretaker brings to you. Giving companionship to someone in need can be a fulfilling and joyful experience. With home caretaking sky rocketing in our country, this will be the future for many of us. Record numbers of Americans are leaving their jobs to take on this responsibility because of the high costs associated with assisted living and nursing homes.

There are many boomers "sandwiched" between the care of aging parents and children. When they leave their jobs to stay home to give care, they create a new sense of purpose, and look for the joy in what they're doing, even though meeting household expenses can be a stretch.

For others, abrupt changes in life are absolutely overwhelming. Sometimes there is no option for you but to be in it. And often, distress is compounded for you because of loss of income from leaving a job, or loss of a marriage or relationship. This wasn't in your future plans for your life. It might be time to consider a new normal.

No matter what the circumstances, you can quickly realize that in caring for someone else, or for pounding the turf for a job, or trying to put yourself back together after the loss of a relationship or loved one, you often lose caring for yourself. Make plans to connect, or reconnect, with others who might have been relegated to the sidelines of your life while you tried to deal with your discouragement, disappointment, or detour.

> *"I can do things you cannot. You can do things I cannot. Together we can do great things."* - Mother Teresa

Connecting with others, whether friends, family, organizations, or support groups, can be an important step to avoiding the toughest parts of the situations I described above. You can feel loneliness, loss of self-esteem, sadness, a lack of confidence, and more. It is so important that you let people into your life, on the telephone, face to face via electronic device, by text, or with a cup of coffee to chat in person. Take every boost you can get. Others will be happy to be in your life even when you are discouraged.

Connection with friends can invigorate you with energy and inspiration. It can lift you up and see your potential. It can appreciate the qualities in you that you may have forgotten.

In addition to the marathons Beth does worldwide, she regularly competes on weekends for fun and practice with her friends and fellow racers. These competitions in Southern California give her instant connection and socializing with a group of people who are like-minded, and whom she knows well.

There are local Challenged Athletes Foundation triathlons and marathons, and she tries to compete in all of them, with occasional down time for resting her body. But in doing these races, she surrounds herself with upbeat friends who are excited to be there.

Fostering and cherishing good relationships can keep you healthy and inspired to keep going when you feel detoured from the life you envisioned for yourself. The reciprocity of giving that inspiration to someone else is a purpose. Connection is crucial for joy in our overloaded, nonstop, fleeting days. Seek it out for your health and happiness. Seek it out for joy. And why not make it your purpose?

Ponder your gifts.

Yes, I believe we all have at least one, and probably more than one. Your gifts drive your purpose. There is no one gift "better than the other." Among my gifts are writing, listening, authenticity, and bringing my best and most understanding self to everyone every day. I know it's a handful, but all of these have been revealed to me as I started to think about why I'm here and what my purpose is.

Beth has numerous gifts. Her incredible gift of athletic ability leads her around the world to be the medium for her gift of spreading joy. Through spreading joy, she is able to use her gift of helping challenged individuals to live joyfully, too.

But mostly, her gift is being able to lift up all of us with kindness, patience, attention and the bright light within her. She believes that her gifts are God-given.

Do you know what your gifts are?

Do you recall the discussion we had about thinking back to being a child in the chapter called "Do You Long to Resurrect a Dream?" This is another time that we might want to revisit our "then" selves. Young children hold so much joy for life and most of us had a dream of what we'd like to be "when we grow up."

Many of us even showed a specific talent that we may or may not have taken into the future. We might have left it behind us as we progressed into future education and training for jobs.

Some of us lost our use of our talents when the growing up process squeezed the "what I want to be when I grow up" out of us. Some of us often used a special gift that was uniquely ours in our family setting and in school.

We can carry that gift with us throughout our lives. As adults, that gift probably takes on a different form than it did as a child, but it utilizes what was an apparent talent to family members, nonetheless.

For some of us, our gift was so vibrant and strong, it was already a purpose just waiting for us to manifest it fully as an adult.

Big or small, your gift is inside you. Sometimes you have to dig for it, because it has been squelched after years of others giving opinions about who you are, what you do, the quality of your work, or any feelings of failure that you've had about all of the above.

You might be surprised, however, that you are already using your gift in what you are doing now.

Like Beth, can you find your gift in your everyday life? Even a tiny morsel of a gift can bring purpose and joy, just as much as a huge windfall.

Consider these as possible gifts that you might have. These are just a few examples:

- Do you have the gift of inspiration? Do you help inspire others?

- Do you have the gift of integrity? Do you take it everywhere?

- How about the gift of motivation? Do you help motivate others to be and do their best?

- Do you have the gift of raising beautiful children, who turn into amazing adults and contribute to the world?

- Maybe your gift is the leadership of a business, employing many in your community?

- Perhaps your gift is steering community organizations, helping others to fulfill their needs and mission?

- Is your gift a donation of your strengths to a charity needing help?

- Do you give the gift of happiness to others as a daily habit?

- Maybe your gift is being authentic throughout all circumstances?

- Are you a wonderful friend to others? Such a gift!

There are so many gifts you might have. We're all different, and no gift is "less" or "more" than any other. Your gifts, whatever they are, can help you set your direction for your purpose and joy, right now, or anytime in the future.

"I say follow your bliss and don't be afraid, and doors will open where you didn't know they were going to be." - Joseph Campbell

Reinvention

Perhaps as you resurrect your purpose and work past your disappointments, discouragements and detours, you feel there is one more step. Might this story about Beth have inspired you to change, to take the first step to reinvent yourself?

We're often "too busy" to give ourselves the space in our lives to create a new purpose, or resurrect a purpose that was detoured, even though we say that we want to. Busyness will not leave room inside us for reinvention. We can be all-consumed with just keeping up with the pace of our overbooked lives with ten to twelve hour workdays, carpooling and homework assistance for the kids, their baseball and football games, lunch engagements, dinner engagements, caretaking for mom and dad, homemaking, yoga classes, spin classes, personal training appointments....Have I said enough?

So, if we truly want to reinvent ourselves to be more of what we envision for our future, we have to make time for it.

Yes, of course, there are many things that are hard to change. For example, you might not be able to cut your work hours. American workers are spending more and more hours at their jobs every year. And more and more of us are foregoing paid vacation time because of the terrible flood in our inboxes that buries us for weeks upon what I call "re-entry." I am so guilty of this. My entire adult life, I have been working too much, yes, too many hours a day. I've worked almost every weekend. The weeks and months fly by, and I realize how much I've missed in the relaxation and "play" department. It's so daunting to think about how we fear just the thing, a vacation, that helps us clear our heads enough to think about the purpose, connections, love, and joy we want in our lives.

For some of you, it might seem impossible. But that doesn't mean you can't envision what you'd love to have in your life, or dream about how you see yourself in the future. Let yourself "feel" what the joy of reinvention would be like.

When Beth resurrected her purpose of helping others, and continued her emphasis on building relationships, the world opened up to her. Everyone supported and enabled her to be a "new" Beth, the same incredible woman, with a now-blockbuster purpose of being a role model for us all. She is helping us see that we can live our dreams, no matter what age, physical condition, or limitations that we have. Her purpose is unstoppable and door-busting.

With her lifelong relationships and her newly found ones as well, she made the leap into global racing. She quickly realized that her presence throughout the world could be life-changing for those who believe they'll never have the life they've wanted. The need for encouragement is everywhere we look. She knows her renewed reason for being here, her renewed and *expanded* purpose. She has found great joy in her global mission.

To reinvent yourself, there might be some things you decide to let go of to leave room for your metamorphosis. These are thoughts, attitudes, and yes, physical clutter.

The letting go process and the joy it allows into your life.

Part of the reinvention process is that of letting go of things that do not add value to your life, but rather, cloud your space and hinder your ability to move forward into the future as you reinvent yourself. What "stuff," emotional and physical, large and small, can you let go of to allow you to reinvent yourself, and to practice your purpose to add joy into your life?

For example, I have been a professional business writer since I was 23. My entire adult life has been driven by deadlines, and when one thing is completed on deadline, another is waiting on my desk with another deadline. As much as I enjoy composition itself, I have never enjoyed the deadlines. It's intense work, and it has caused many a long night falling asleep at the computer. Sleep studies now show that I am a perfect candidate for a shorter life span because of lack of ZZZZZZs. Ouch! I figured with all of the sleep I've lacked in my adult life, I was a goner.

So, in the past year, I have come to re-evaluate my life. I finally decided to reduce my deadlines. I was ready to let that life go. I started thinking about how, at the rate I was working, life would race past me without joy and purpose. That hit home. I wanted reinvention.

Once I made this decision, joy overcame me. I still do plenty of work, but I now have time to tend flowers and enjoy my veranda. I have unhurried time to spend with my husband. I plan longer trips to see my family in other states. I have a renewed purpose of connection. This gave happiness and joy room to appear and grow. I gave them space to thrive.

Here are some ways to kickstart your reinvention process:

- Dream about anything and everything. Your dreams are yours. No one can stop them or take them away. Daydream to visualize yourself in the future, or to create a "new you."

- Change your attitude and it changes everything. This one works wonders. It takes only one tiny change in attitude and perspective at a time to create another tiny change, and another, and another, and another. You can be a completely different person as these tiny changes create a new you on the inside and out. It's a great step toward reinvention.

- Let the small stuff go. This can even mean cleaning out the clutter in your home, thus cleaning out the clutter in your brain. My office is the home of my clutter. Cleaning it out is the best! My purpose is clear, and when I achieve success with piles of stuff on the shredder and in the trash can, I am proud of myself and joyful. It sounds really dumb, right? Try it.

- Immerse yourself in studying material that will give you ideas on how to initiate your desired changes, big or small, and feed your appetite for improvement throughout your journey. It can be anything you'd like. Access to great reading, viewing and listening arriers anymore. There is plenty of help for and resurrecting purpose.

Hire a coach, whether a life coach, an executive coach, a personal branding coach, or a job search coach. If you feel like you need solid one-on-one help with creating your path to becoming the "you" you want to be going forward, check this out. Some coaches can be extremely helpful in making steps for you to take.

- Be authentically you. This creates meaning in your life and is the way to be true to yourself. When we are authentic, it attracts others who are authentic, and it enriches your life. They will be supportive as you grow and reinvent toward fulfilling your purpose.

Authenticity does not necessarily come from an ivy-league education, or being the top dog at a corporation. It does not have an expiration date. It doesn't fade away, never to be found again. We can reinvigorate it any time we would like. Reinvention of ourselves is a great time to do it.

Think back again to your childhood and the dreams you had for a purpose. It's a place where you might find the roots of your authenticity. Extract them to refresh and renew them right where you are.

Many of us have buried our authenticity because of work a home situations, negative relationships, or embarrassment at some point in our lives when we were completely ourselves. Don't worry. We all stumble. It's a part of being authentic.

As you reinvent yourself, share your stories of embarrassment or failure. Embrace them! People are drawn to others' foibles and imperfections, particularly if you tell your stories with humor and sincerity. They respect you more for feeling comfortable enough to tell them.

Authenticity can be developed just like any other of your talents or characteristics. It can grow and change and be stronger as *you* grow and change. It is a critical component of your metamorphosis in reinvention. That's why I discuss it here.

It is, in fact, an excellent tool for reinvention as you define yourself with your purpose. Whether you're reinventing yourself with a new purpose, or making a commitment to resurrect an existing purpose to continue in your life as it is now, authenticity is important for joy, relationships, and love.

Be true to your authentic self every day, and see how much other people respect you and may want to be around you. Authenticity can bring you love, and helps you to return it and spread it. And, more importantly, your authentic self makes it a delight for you to spend time with *yourself*.

Your reinvention will appear from the inside-out. First, you make your changes on the inside, and soon they will be visible on the outside.

> *"Inside yourself or outside, you never have to change what you see, only the way you see it."*
> - Thaddeus Golas

Let your hope for your purpose and joy live.

How has Beth, this amazing lady, affected how you feel about your own goals, purpose, future, and search for joy? Does she inspire you to hold on to hope?

Perhaps, like many of us at some point in our lives, you have been through disappointments, discouragements, or detours that have challenged you beyond ways that you could have ever foreseen.

Like Beth, perhaps you experienced a tragic accident. Possibly it left you disabled or brain damaged. Maybe you were born with a debilitating physical condition. Perchance you are a warrior wounded in a conflict. You might need inspiration! Beth has the qualities of a genuine survivor who is living her purpose with pure joy. She is here to help you by telling her story.

Can you imagine the hopefulness of Beth and her family after her tragedy? Can you imagine how strong with hope they must have been in every moment of the day? Hope is a powerful life force of joyful and purpose driven living. The first step is to revive your hopes for your present and your future. Articulate them. Write them down. Read them every day, like an affirmation. Hope is meant to be a day-to-day part of your life.

It's an essential part of you. Hope has lifted up and propelled many to their dreams and purposes throughout history. Your hope can do that for you as well. Hope for the future, and your dreams of renewed purpose, can lead you to create an improved life for yourself, one that makes the good parts better, increases your love and joy, and fosters relationships. Ultimately, if you wish, they can result in your reinvention.

My hope for you is that Beth Sanden's life has touched you, inspired you, and motivated you to resurrect your own purpose and live it. Or perhaps *her* life has set you on the journey to *discover* your purpose, and to continue on to reinvent yourself.

Now, it's your turn to break through your disappointments, discouragements, and detours to resurrect *your* purpose and live it.

"The grand essentials of happiness are: something to do, something to love, and something to hope for." - Alexander Chalmers

Beth has begun racing "Triple 7s." She started in Africa: 7 marathons / in 7 days / in 7 different African countries. She raced in South Africa, Lesotho, Swaziland, Namibia, Zimbabwe, Zambia, and Botswana. The races were planned for July 30th through August 5th, 2017. There was, however, a twist in the schedule. There was an interesting change. It is another tale to tell.

She also celebrated her 63rd birthday while there. The story about this great lady continues ....

"New dreams, new works in progress. That's the ticket for a long and happy ride." - George Burns